THE ECONOMIC THOUGHT OF KARL POLANYI

Also by J. R. Stanfield

THE ECONOMIC SURPLUS AND NEO-MARXISM

ECONOMIC THOUGHT AND SOCIAL CHANGE

THE ECONOMIC THOUGHT OF KARL POLANYI

Lives and Livelihood

J. R. Stanfield

St. Martin's Press New York

First published in the United States of America in 1986

Printed in Hong Kong

ISBN 0–312–23658–1

Library of Congress Cataloging-in-Publication Data
Stanfield, J. Ron, 1945–
The economic thought of Karl Polanyi.
Includes index.
1. Polanyi, Karl, 1886–1964. 2. Economists—Hungary.
I. Title.
HB102.P64S73 1986 330.1 85–27785
ISBN 0–312–23658–1

For Jackie, Bailey and Kellin,
who teach me every day about life and livelihood

Contents

Preface

By this book I seek to draw attention to the possibility and necessity of an economics that is more existential and human-centred than the conventional economics. Karl Polanyi did not underestimate the significance of livelihood to lives; he recognized that an inadequate quantity of the former is detrimental to the quality of the latter. He emphasized nonetheless that beyond sufficient livelihood preoccupation with more economic wealth greatly erodes the quality of human existence. An economics and a larger culture that puts the economy in its proper subordinate place in human society are required to locate the golden mean that avoids the debilitating consequences of meagreness as well as the humiliating enslavement to avariciousness. For me, the work of Karl Polanyi is an excellent start toward a new way of thinking about the economy and its place in society, of lives and livelihood.

For convenience, throughout the book I have used parenthetical abbreviations for several books written by Polanyi or the Polanyi Group. They are:

GT	Karl Polanyi, *The Great Transformation* (Boston: Beacon Press, 1957; originally published in 1944).
TMEE	Karl Polanyi, Conrad M. Arensberg and Harry W. Pearson (eds), *Trade and Market in the Early Empires* (Chicago: Henry Regnery, 1971, originally published in 1957).
DST	Karl Polanyi in collaboration with Abraham Rotstein, *Dahomey and the Slave Trade* (Seattle: University of Washington Press, 1966).
PAME	George Dalton (ed.), *Primitive, Archaic, and Modern Economies: Essays of Karl Polanyi* (Garden City, NY: Doubleday, 1968).
LM	Karl Polanyi (Harry W. Pearson, ed.), *The Livelihood of Man* (New York: Academic Press, 1977).

TPE	George Dalton (ed.), *Tribal and Peasant Economies* (Austin: University of Texas Press, 1967).
EDSC	George Dalton (ed.), *Economic Development and Social Change* (Garden City, New York: Natural History Press, 1971).
SAE	Marshall Sahlins, *Stone Age Economics* (Chicago: Aldine, 1974).

In the necessary endeavour of trying to acknowledge those who contributed to this effort, I face a formidable task because they are so many and I needed so much help. For discussion and suggestions, I thank Ray Benton, Terry Neale, Ernie Diedrich, Doug Brown, Bill Kern, Rich Stratton, Bruce McDaniel, Bill Dugger, Anne Mayhew, Bud Hartman, Lee Gray, Hal Cochrane, and Bob Keller. For sharing unpublished manuscripts with me, I thank George Dalton and Fred Block. I took the inspiration for the book's title from Peter Drucker who observed that Polanyi was one of the few since the young Marx to raise the question of the relationship between 'livelihood', the economy, and 'lives', or the community. Special thanks go to Al Eichner for his valuable interest and suggestions and to Kari Polanyi-Levitt for helping me to avoid the more egregious errors in the biographical synopsis of Polanyi. Some of the chapters in the book reuse or are based on articles published previously in the *Journal of Economic Issues* and the *International Journal of Social Economics*. I appreciate the typists who are the really productive people in this project: Willa Hintergardt, Gwendolyn Ruffin, and Waneta Boyce. Finally, there are Jackie, Bailey, and Kellin, and I have already said in the dedication that for which I profoundly thank them.

1 The Life and Work of Karl Polanyi

Although my principal concern in this book is developing the ideas of Karl Polanyi for their significance to the practice of economics and everyday life in the democratic industrial societies, a book such as this one is by its very nature to some extent an exercise in the history of ideas. Therefore, in this initial chapter I treat Polanyi from that perspective, i.e. I attempt to convey an impression of the man, his times, and his place in the evolution of social and economic thought. I first briefly review his life and attempt to convey something of his nature. Secondly, and thirdly, I summarize his intellectual antecedents or influences and the influence he has to date exercised on other scholars. The discussion of his influence is particularly synoptic and intentionally suggestive with no pretense of being definitive. There are several reasons for this. His principal influence thus far is in anthropology, not in my chosen field of economics. His influence is only now developing outside anthropology and therefore difficult and fruitless to assess in detail. Finally, exhaustive treatment of the matter of Polanyi's present influence would carry me too far afield from my main purpose in the book: interpreting the thrust of his work and arguing that it should be much more influential in the practice of economics and everyday life.

BIOGRAPHICAL NOTES[1]

Karl Polanyi was born in Vienna on 21 October 1886, to intensely intellectual and politically concerned parents whose children inherited all their fervour. Polanyi's father, Mihály Pollacsek, birthdate uncertain, was born into a Jewish bourgeois family in the town of Ungvar, then located in a Hungarian province, now in Slovakia.

Although he later converted his wife and children to Protestantism and Magyarized their names to Polanyi, he located his family in Budapest's Jewish intellectual community. Pollacsek studied engineering in Zurich and undertook a highly successful career building railroads. After his return to Hungary, he pursued his railroad enterprises with great success and became quite wealthy by the standard for a commoner in nineteenth-century Hungary. His enterprises collapsed shortly after 1900 and he was virtually bankrupt when he died in 1906. Much of his poverty stemmed from his insistence that the shareholders and creditors of his enterprises be reimbursed.

Karl Polanyi's mother, Cecile Wohl, was the daughter of a Russian rabbinical scholar in Vilna. She may have met her husband-to-be in Switzerland, her travels there and her living in Vienna under the guardianship of Samuel Klatschko having resulted from her father's fear that she would be arrested for her association with *narodniki*. Her wit and intellect are generally reported, but to some she turned these talents toward shrewishness, to others, gaiety. At any rate, her salon appears to have been a popular gathering place for Budapest's intellectual *avant garde*. One frequent visitor was fellow Vilna townsman Klatschko, himself an exiled Russian *narodnik*, whose rebel's courage and populist views entertained and no doubt influenced Polanyi.

Polanyi's siblings are no less remarkable for their abilities and struggles. To escape the hypocritical, corrupt influence of society, the children were given an eccentric education patterned after the notions of Rousseau and James Mill. Adolph followed his father's lead into engineering and railroad building, with a successful career in Japan, Italy, and especially Brazil, where he developed a strong and perhaps influential interest in that country's political and cultural life. Laura, known familiarly as Mausi, was associated with the Central European folk movement that produced the music of Bela Bartok and influential political figures such as Josip Broz, who became Yugoslavia's Marshall Tito, and Franz Oppenheimer, designer of Israel's *kibbutzim*. The youngest child, Michael, is easily the most famous of the Polanyi children. He began a promising career in physical chemistry, but the characteristic Polanyi interest in politics and the humanities asserted itself and he turned to philosophy, where his contribution to the theory of knowledge have achieved widespread recognition. Michael and Karl were both influenced by, and influential in, not only the interwar period's intense interest in the sociology of knowledge but also the contemporaneous debate on planning and freedom.

Karl, born between Laura and Michael, was raised in Budapest and began his law studies at the University of Budapest. The official curriculum there was political economy and constitutional history, but the students devoted much extracurricular study to Marxism and sociology. For Polanyi, these extracurricular topics would have been a continuance of the heady discussions his mother hosted. Karl was expelled from Budapest over differences, indeed a fist fight, with more conservative students and finished his degree at Kolozsvar. He served as a clerk in a law office from 1910 and was called to the bar in 1912 in Budapest. He practised law for a short time but apparently did so in erstwhile fashion, ever ready to take time off for intellectual and political pursuits.

Of Karl Polanyi it is often noted that, though a lifelong socialist, he was basically apolitical. His early career apparently belies the latter characterization. While still in high school, under the influence of Klatschko, he joined a socialist students' organization. While a law student at Budapest, he may have assisted the wealthy aristocrat, Count Mihály Károlyi, in the formation of the short-lived Hungarian Liberal Party. Polanyi was early on associated with Oszkár Jászi, the co-leader with Károlyi of the short-lived democratic government in 1918. Polanyi had responded to Jászi's 1913 call for the formation of a radical party to unify the dissenting elements of the intelligentsia, middle class, peasantry, and non-Magyar minorities. The National Citizens' Radical Party was formally chartered in June 1914, two months before the assassination that plunged Europe into war. The party's programme was important in the Károlyi–Jászi government, though perhaps not dominant since the governing coalition included Hungarian socialists who were wedded to Marxism and reluctant to embrace the peasant alliance and folk culture populism of the Citizens' Party. At any rate, the coalition's stalemate contributed to the takeover by the Hungarian Communist Party led by Béla Kun that quelched the democratic experiment in less than a year. The Hungarian Soviet Republic was itself short-lived, replaced by a right-wing government. Polanyi, ailing from war wounds and perhaps sensing the imminent collapse of the left, took refuge in Vienna even before the fall of Kun's government.

Also while still a student in Budapest, in 1908, Polanyi was a founder and first president of the Galilei Circle, a political and intellectual club from which many liberal and socialist figures of interwar Hungary were drawn. The general background of the Galilei Circle was the counter-cultural movement of *fin de siècle* Budapest to which many of Cecile Wohl Polanyi's salon guests had contributed. This movement was dedicated to providing a rekindled cultural atmosphere to replace the stifling orthodoxy of Christianity and nationalism imposed by the Magyar aristocracy. The movement encompassed the sociologist Jaszi, the composer Bartok, the Freudian psychoanalyst Sandor Ferenczi, literary figures, and artists influenced by the French Impressionists. The poet Endre Ady spoke for the movement when he challenged the authority of the aristocracy on the grounds of moral dereliction and called for a national regeneration based on moral principles and the noble traditions of Hungarian common culture. Recalling the founding of the Circle in a 1929 memoir, Polanyi noted its relation to the decadent moral atmosphere of Hungarian public life:

> For generations, moral standards were not imperative in Hungarian public life. The representatives of the working-class, whom the Hungarian moral quagmire finally entrapped, had also sunk into a profitable, or at least a comfortable opportunism. The Galilei Circle took upon itself that without which life becomes ignominious; self-sacrificing responsibility for the rights of others. . . . The Galilei Circle's assets were moral.[2]

If moral regeneration was the Circle's fundamental goal, its immediate concern was academic and scientific freedom. A University of Budapest professor named Gyula Pikler, who was very popular among liberal-minded students, was singled out for harassment by university officials and conservative students. Pikler, though not especially active politically, held inconvenient views with scholarly conviction. He taught that laws and social institutions were historically relative, subject to revision as the perceived needs of society changed. Such relativism, while far short of radical constructivism, found little favour in the anachronistic, absolutist atmosphere of the Hapsburg aristocracy. The students who came successfully to Pikler's defence decided to give permanent expression to their unity by forming the Circle. The Circle's announced aim was to defend academic and scientific freedom in the struggle against religious, racial, and class prejudices. It sponsored a lecture series visited not only by Pikler, Jászi, and Ferenczi, but also by such notable foreign scholars as Max Adler, Werner Sombart, and

Eduard Bernstein. Adolph Polanyi and Georg Lukacs lectured in the Circle's programme in the spring of 1909. The Circle also established reading rooms and published scholarly materials with particular emphasis on contributions by young scholars.

The Circle's defence of academic and scientific freedom was not apolitical. The intent was to build a bridge toward a broadly encompassing and generally distributed civil rights. The Circle was heavily engaged in outreach activities to the working class, and members gave frequent lectures to trade unions, a practice Polanyi was later to continue in England. The Circle's ambition was not veiled; it annually celebrated, with lectures and poems composed for the occasions by Ady, the March Laws. The March Laws were adopted as a step toward constitutional government by the Hungarian lower house in 15 March 1848.

This youthful political activity may only apparently belie Polanyi's oft-noted apolitical nature. Recalling the Circle in a letter about a half century later, he himself remarked on its success in the moral education of its members and its utter failure in terms of practical political action. Indeed, Polanyi and his fellow Circle members affirmed Jászi's view that 'politics was not a matter of business or elocution, but a means of bringing about a more fully-developed morality'.[3] Polanyi took responsibility for the Circle's failure to be ready to lead a liberal political movement when the opportunity presented itself in 1918, lamenting his antipolitical leadership and remarking that 'I have never been a politician, I had no talent that way, no interest even' (*LM*, p. xiv).

Polanyi's socialism was similarly more the conclusion of a humanist scholar than a matter of practical political action. This was evident even in his early contribution (1922) to the debate on economic calculation in a socialist society.[4] In that article he focused more on the moral superiority of socialism and its relation to the quality of social life than on the politics of creating socialism or the possibilities of economic calculation in a socialist economy. Here again is affirmation of Jászi's view of politics as a process of moral education. For Polanyi, as his daughter observed,

> socialism is not better because it is technologically more efficient – although it may well prove to be so – but because only under socialism does it become possible to subordinate the technological and economic order to social and human requirements.[5]

Only socialism can overcome the demoralized atmosphere of market capitalist society with its disembedded economy and permit 'the transcending of an industrial civilization through a deliberate subordination of the economy to the ends of the human community'.[6] This was the radicalism of Owen and Marx: 'they both built their thought structures on the reality of society and the conviction that the future of man depends on his adapting his institutions radically to the nature of the machine, within the limits of the laws governing real social existence'.[7] Such has also always been the clarion call of institutional economics.

Polanyi's political and legal career was interrupted in 1914 by World War I in which he served as a cavalry officer in the Austro–Hungarian army. He was badly wounded on the Galician front and returned to Budapest in 1917. In 1919, his war ailments led to his hospitalization in Vienna for major surgery. There he met, or most likely became reacquainted with, Ilona Ducyznska, whom he subsequently married in 1923. Ilona was from an old Hungarian gentry family. Although considerably younger than Polanyi, she already had a substantial record of political activism when they met. Indeed, after her return from studying abroad, she introduced a more activist political, antiwar spirit into the Galilei Circle. She was arrested for antiwar activities in 1917 and was a member of the Communist Party while it was still underground. She played some role in the Hungarian revolution of 1918, and fled to Vienna upon the collapse of the Hungarian Soviet Republic.

From 1924 to 1933, Polanyi served as associate editor and feature analytical writer on the staff of *Der Osterreichische Volkswirt* or *The Austrian Economist*, a periodical which has been compared to *The London Economist* and *The Wall Street Journal*. In this capacity Polanyi kept abreast of the world political economic events and anticipated in his writings the major changes to come in Stalin's USSR, Chiang-Kai Shek's China, and Keynes' depressed capitalism. Polanyi now followed as a journalist the disruption of lives by economic insecurity and crisis and political stalemate and instability that he had experienced directly as a young adult. This disruption, eventually taking focus as the problem of lives and livelihood, became the central concern of his later work in political economy. Polanyi was well paid for this work with the *Austrian Economist*, but he, Ilona, their young daughter, and Ilona's widowed mother did not live as comfortably as they might have because much of his earnings were donated to refugee relief.

Polanyi lost his job with the *Austrian Economist* in 1933. Sales had fallen as a result of the Great Depression, especially given the Nazi's ban of the periodical in Germany. In 1933, in light of the rising tide of Austrian fascism, Polanyi emigrated to England where he made a precarious living for the next few years lecturing for the Workers' Educational Association that was organized under the auspices of the extramural departments of Oxford University and the University of London. He also toured the United States on occasion in this period, lecturing in as many thirty-eight states. In 1940, while on such a trip, Polanyi was precluded from returning to his family in England by the blitzkrieg. He stayed with Peter Drucker and continued to give guest lectures. Through Drucker, Polanyi received a visiting scholar's appointment at Bennington College in Vermont where from 1941 to 1943 he wrote *The Great Transformation*. Ilona eventually joined him and taught physics at Bennington. In 1943 they returned to England.

After the war, Polanyi was appointed Visiting Professor of Economics at Columbia University. The family home was moved to Pickering near Toronto because Ilona was denied a US visa on the basis of her youthful Communist Party activities. Polanyi taught from 1947 to 1953 at Columbia, and his General Economic History course was immensely popular and influential. After his retirement in 1953, he continued his association with Columbia for several years as Adjunct Professor of Economics, principally engaged as a co-director (with Conrad Arensberg) of the Interdisciplinary Project on the Institutional Aspects of Economic Growth. From this project emerged *Trade and Market in the Early Empires* and the influence of the Polanyi Group in economic anthropology.

Polanyi's final major project was the founding of *Co-Existence*, an interdisciplinary journal for the comparative study of economics and politics, dedicated to the cause of world peace through knowledge of the realities of cultural differences and the unity of the human condition. After organizing a distinguished editorial board and seeing the first issue to the printer, Polanyi died on 23 April 1964, literally days before the first copies appeared. His daughter, Kari Levitt, wrote a review of Polanyi's efforts to found *Co-Existence* for the second number of the journal in November 1964.

INFLUENCES

Certainly Aristotle must be mentioned first as a preliminary influence on Polanyi. Indeed, Polanyi's appreciation of Aristotle is virtually boundless. He viewed the seminal Greek philosopher as having addressed 'the problem of man's livelihood with a radicalism of which no later writer on the subject was capable – none has ever penetrated deeper into the material organization of man's life. In effect, he posed, in all its breadth, the question of the place occupied by economy in society' (*TMEE*, p. 66). Elsewhere, Polanyi said that Aristotle's 'famous distinction of householding proper and money making . . . was probably the most prophetic pointer ever made in the realm of the social sciences; it is certainly still the best analysis of the subject we possess' (*GT*. pp. 53–4).

Polanyi saw a portent paradox in Aristotle's relative neglect at the hands of modern economists *vis-à-vis* his influence in other modern disciplines and on pre-capitalistic economics, this neglect despite Aristotle's having devoted a great deal of attention to the economy (*TMEE*, p. 65). This paradox may have led Polanyi to search for a cause, and this cause may have paved the way for his interpretation of market capitalism as a disembedded economy and of his discussion of the enthnocentrism of the formalist perspective. For Polanyi, a key point was that Greek society was not at that time a market economy, 'rather, they were latecomers in a civilized marketless world, and compelled by circumstances to become pioneers in the development of the novel trading methods which were at most on the point of turning towards market trade' (*TMEE*, p. 67). Thusly placed, Aristotle's focus was on trade and prices *vis-à-vis* his conception of the economy. Here we find the roots of Polanyi's substantivism as well as his notion of the disembedded economy. Aristotle denied universal scarcity, which is of course the basis of formalism. For Aristotle, 'man, like any other animal, was presented . . . as naturally self-sufficient. The human economy did not, therefore, stem from the boundlessness of man's wants and needs, or, as it is phrased today, from the fact of scarcity' (*TMEE*, p. 66). Here we also find an intimation of Polanyi's empirical and cultural or social approach to human behaviour rather than a deductive and psychological approach. For Aristotle, wants originate in the social process or cultural context and no mere psychological postulate of scarcity which identifies man as a creature with boundless wants can serve social analysis. Boundless wants, in Aristotle's view, represent a cultural distortion rather than a fact given by any naturally acquisitive character of men *vis-à-vis* a niggardly nature (*TMEE*, pp. 80–3).

The source of this cultural distortion was an institutional configuration that made economic wealth appear to be an end in itself. This occurs, in Aristotle's view, in the marketeer's mentality because here gain itself is the purpose of trade. For Aristotle, natural exchange is exchange that is oriented towards provisioning the wants of the parties involved. Since natural wants are limited by the means–ends relations, natural exchange is similarly bounded. Economic wealth is here viewed as a means to an end, and it is then bounded by its relation to that end. Unnatural exchange is not so bounded because there is no finite limit to the accumulation of wealth in the abstract, that is, monetary wealth. Aristotle foresaw the characteristic defect of market society before seeing such a society because he was not blinded by the power of unnatural exchange and its associated lust to fuel economic development. As Polanyi noted, 'in the absence of price-making markets he [Aristotle] would have seen nothing but perversity in the expectation that the new urge for money making might conceivably serve a useful purpose' (*TMEE*, p. 87).

Here also lies an intimation of Polanyi's pivotal concept of the disembedded economy. Aristotle was faced with the policy and everyday practical problem of trade and pricing in the social economic process. His substantive view of the economy led him to view trade and pricing in relation to social reproduction. That is to say, these two practical problems, trade and pricing, required for their analysis a standard of evaluation. For Aristotle this standard of evaluation was instrumental in character, being primarily oriented to the reproduction of society.

> Unless the question of commercial trade and the setting of prices could be linked to the requirements of communal existence and its self-sufficiency, there was no rational way of judging of either, be it in theory or in practice. If such a link did offer, then the answer was simple: first, trade that served to restore self-sufficiency was "in accordance with nature"; trade that did not, was "contrary to nature." Second, prices should be such as to strengthen the bond of community; otherwise exchange will not continue to take place and the community will cease to exist. The mediating concept was in either case the self-sufficiency of the economy. (*TMEE*, p. 82)

Natural exchange was then a way of sharing between producers so as to allow division of labour and security of reproduction. Justice in exchange relations was fundamentally necessary to avoid conflict and sustain exchange. 'That which insures justice, whether in regard to the distribution of the prizes of life or the adjudication of conflicts, or the regulation of mutual services is good since it is required for the continuance of the group' (*TMEE*, p. 79). In Aristotle's view, society is superordinate to the economy because society culturally determines what should be reproduced and what is just. This social determination dominates the exchange process. Unnatural exchange, aimed at money making pure and simple rather than reproducing a community and sustaining amicable relations, is the root of Polanyi's concept of the disembedded economy.

This is not to suggest that Polanyi gleaned his visions of the substantive view and the disembedded economy from Aristotle alone; the intermediaries were numerous and significant. The medieval world view, even before it obtained an Aristotelian hue because of the influence of Aquinas, was thoroughly solidaristic and reproductive in its view of the economy. Early Christian doctrine is replete with concern for the morality of gain and usury, the souls of the professional trader and man of wealth, justice in pricing, and so on. This line of thought is best understood in light of the economic conception of materially reproducing society while maintaining the reciprocal goodwill of its constituent families and individuals. The economy here is still viewed as a set of morally bounded relations between people; only in seventeenth-century England does the contrary notion of a disembedded economy make its abrupt and fateful appearance.[8] A century later Smith provided his grand synthesis with which some of his followers consummated the rise of the disembedded economy in theory and practice (see *GT*, ch. 10). In Polanyi's interpretation, despite the emphasis given to depoliticizing the economy, the economy remains subordinate to society in Smith's thinking because self-interest is guided by the fundamental dignity of man as a moral and social being seeking to gain the approval of his fellows. In Polanyi's view, the decisive hand is Townsend's, because his naturalism led subsequent classical economists to demoralize the economy. For Polanyi, the twentieth century necessarily struggles to remoralize and repoliticize the economy.

That Polanyi refuses to place mercantilism in a path of logical historical development to market capitalism (*GT*, p. 67) suggests he may have been influenced to some extent by such thinkers as Sir James Steuart, who coined the term political economy and defined it thusly: 'oeconomy, in general, is the art of providing for all the wants of a family with prudence and frugality. . . . What oeconomy is in a family, political oeconomy is in a state'.[9] As some writers have suggested, there may have been more to the mercantilist line of thought that emphasized state administration than the subordination of economy to the glory and power of the state.[10] That is, this thought may have contained some sort of social integrity or social welfare view. Either way, this element of mercantilism certainly viewed the economy as subordinate to social and political purposes, and in that sense it was part of a continuity of thought from the Greek and medieval world views, notwithstanding the sharp break that other mercantilists made in paving the way for the market mentality.

Beyond classical economics this view found expression in various Romanticist, fascist, historicist, and institutionalist writings. It is difficult to know which of these may have influenced Polanyi directly or indirectly. He himself cites Hegel, Marx, Maine, Tönnies, Weber, and Malinowski as pivotal to his conception of the disembedded economy (*TMEE*, pp. 68–70). In addition to these scholars, the debt his economic anthropology owes to Bücher, Durkheim, and Thurnwald is clear enough. Certainly these scholars, along with Aristotle, are sufficient ground for Polanyi's central theme that market economy remakes society, in the process destroying solidarity and destabilizing the substantive economy thereby ultimately threatening social disintegration. This theme is found in the other traditions mentioned above, notably so in the Romantic scholars such as Carlyle and Ruskin. Polanyi seems to have developed his notion of a spontaneous counter-response to this social disintegration without influence by the American institutionalists, such as Walton Hamilton, who also promoted it.

Among the so-called utopian socialists, Robert Owen is singled out by Polanyi as having been particularly influential. Indeed, his praise of Owen is perhaps as lavish as that he accorded Aristotle. 'One man alone perceived the meaning of the ordeal, perhaps because amongst the leading spirits of the age he alone possessed intimate practical knowledge of industry and was also open to inner vision. No thinker ever advanced farther than Robert Owen did into the realm of industrial society' (*GT*, p. 127).

Polanyi credits Owen with discovering the reality of society (*GT*, p. 128), a reality which Polanyi describes as one of the three constitutive facts of Western consciousness and which he posed so forcefully opposite the disembedded economy. 'That human possibilities were limited, not by the laws of the market, but by those of society itself was a recognition reserved to Owen who alone discerned behind the veil of market economy the emergent reality: society' (*GT*, p. 85). According to Polanyi, Owen rejected Christianity because of the narrow individualism inherent in its view of the individual's responsibility for his own character. Such a doctrine Owen saw as contrary to the reality of society. For Polanyi the essence of Owen's denial of Christianity 'lay in his insistence on the social origin of human motives' (*GT*, p. 128).

In this social reality Polanyi also saw Owen refusing to cordon off the economic sphere, insisting instead on discussing man as a whole and evincing a concern for the wholeness of life. With one foot in the medieval world view of 'corporative life' (*GT*, p. 169), 'the strength of Owenism was that its inspiration was eminently practical, and yet its methods were based on an appreciation of man as a whole' (*GT*, p. 167). This 'distinctive trait' in Owenism, its social or holistic approach, enabled it to see problems of industrial civilization not primarily in economic but in social terms (*GT*, p. 170). Owen's 'genius recognized that the incorporation of the machine was possible only in a new society. The industrial aspect of things was to him in no way restricted to the economic (this would have implied a marketing view of society which he rejected)' (*GT*, p. 170). A key theme of Polanyi is that a social transformation, that is, the building of a new society, is necessary if mankind is to retain its humanity and achieve wholeness and fullness of life in an industrial society.

There is also in Owen's insights the malleable human character that Polanyi was later to lay as a cornerstone of his inquiry. Institutional analysis is for Polanyi more sociological than psychological because it is the institutions that surround an individual's actions that mould his character. At any given time the persistence and importance of this or that propensity in basic human nature is determined by the institutional milieu which supports or promotes some elements of the human potential and represses other elements.

In specific terms, Owen saw the spread of gain-oriented activity bringing about a fundamental change in character. A key defect of market capitalism for Polanyi, as for Tawney in the wake of Ruskin, was its reliance on gain or acquisition as a fundamental motivating force. This 'humiliating enslavement to the "material"' was the root of Tawney's '"sickness of an acquisitive society"' (*PAME*, p. 72). Owen foresaw the rise of a new character as a necessary result of the defusion of the gain motive, and he also foresaw consequences of this change in 1817 which for Polanyi 'described the course on which Western man had entered and his words summed up the problem of the coming century' (*GT*, p. 128). Owen argued that this new character 'is formed upon a principle quite unfavourable to individual or general happiness, it will produce the most lamentable and permanent evils, unless its tendency be counteracted by legislative interference and direction' (*GT*, p. 128). Here Owen introduces the notion of a protective response, later to be a major theme of Polanyi's work.

In this vein, Owen also saw that the crisis of market capitalism was not narrowly economic but of profoundly wider compass. It was a cultural crisis, reaching into the way men assign meanings to their lives. Owen emphasized not incomes but degradation and misery (*GT*, p. 129). According to Polanyi, Owen taught his workers that degradation stemmed from a cultural vacuum in which their lives had lost their meaning (*GT*, p. 158). From such degradation, Owen continued, high wages alone would not provide salvation because income must be meaningfully spent if it is to serve the requirements of a humane existence (*GT*, p. 293). Because meaning and motivation derive from culture, the patterned social interaction of a human group, the disruption of those patterns without adequate compensation from new institutions leads to a moral lacuna in the nature of Durkheim's anomie. This is of signal importance to Polanyi because to him market capitalism caused a 'social calamity [that] is primarily a cultural not an economic phenomenon that can be measured by income figures or population statistics' (*GT*, p. 157). The true basis of criticism of market capitalism and the degradation it spawns must always be transeconomic.

> Not economic exploitation, as often assumed, but the disintegration of the cultural environment of the victim is then the cause of the degradation. The economic process may, naturally, supply the vehicle of the destruction, and almost invariably economic inferiority will make the weaker yield, but the immediate cause of his undoing is not for that reason economic; it lies in the lethal injury to the institutions in which his social existence is embodied.

> The result is loss of self-respect and standards, whether the unit is a people or a class, whether the process springs from so-called "culture conflict", or from a change in the position of a class within the confines of a society. (*GT*, p. 157)

Polanyi went on to discuss the cultural crisis of Africa in what must be one of the earliest statements as to the true cost of Western imperialism.

I think Polanyi may overstate the originality of Owen. Godwin and others of the Enlightenment stress the malleability of human character and the defeat of humanity's essential goodness by exploitative institutions. Marx most certainly had a broader view of the human misery of capitalism than is suggested by some discussion of exploitation and increasing misery. Nonetheless, Polanyi may have learned these things from Owen. It must be said then that if from Aristotle Polanyi learned that the function of the economy is to provision society, from Owen he learned that an economy not subordinate to this purpose disrupts the very lives it is meant to serve.

To these intellectual antecedents must be added the influence of earlier acquaintances and the life events sketched above. Polanyi's commitment to the sociological view reflects not only the influence of Pikler and Jaszi but also the extracurricular, avant-garde concern with Marxism and the new discipline of sociology. Pikler's teachings on the adjustment of law and institutions to better serve the perceived needs of a given human group at a given time would have given academic vitality to the reform spirit that Polanyi had always lived with in his family setting. Sociology was an approach taken by those in the interwar period who wished to understand the general cultural crisis of the European order. Its characteristic focus at the time was on the sociology of knowledge and the way in which people come to understand their life events and their position in them. The economic crisis of the interwar period and the development of Soviet socialism would have created even more interest in Marx's critical analysis of capitalism and in the possibilities of the socialist alternative.

Polanyi's frequent insistence on the reality of society is reminiscent of similar concerns in Marx and Owen. Polanyi leaned toward Owen in this regard because he detected a fatalistic determinism in Marxism. It should be noted that Polanyi, especially in his later academic writings, often distinguished Marx from his followers. This no doubt reflects Polanyi's friendship with his fellow Hungarian, Georg Lukacs, whose work did much to bring about the cultural or humanistic Marxism, now ascendant, that vastly softens the economic determinism of Marxist theory. Still, Owen's approach is similar to the concerns of the Galilei Circle with moral and individual responsibility. For Polanyi the example of the poet Ady may have been decisive in this regard. In his 1919 eulogy for the poet, Polanyi referred to Ady's example to the young generation of Hungary. Polanyi lamented the deterministic nature of many radicals at the time, avowing that they were convinced that social reality and circumstances determine the course of history as if the men involved were but pawns in the grip of inexorable forces. Polanyi rhetorically asked why do so many honour such men as Ady who champion a belief in individual responsibility and self sacrifice and answered that men do so because they secretly believe that the idealists such as Ady are right. Polanyi continued that the truth is 'that the bird soars despite rather than because of the law of gravity' and 'that society soars to stages embodying ever loftier ideals despite rather than because of material interest'.[11] Polanyi's reality of society was never used to deny the reality of the soul or the spirit or the necessity of individual responbility and ethical concern.

Thus, for Polanyi, historical materialism, despite its methodical significance to economic history and sociology, provided absolutely no basis for philosophy or practical ethics. He saw Marxism, with its inexorable historical progression, as viewing the world from outside rather than inside. Such a vision is directly contrary to one of Polanyi's most insistent messages: the human economy is a set of moral relations that must be studied by people operating within those relations. The necessary lesson involved is that the theory of value must be focused not on how prices are formed out there in some autonomous market process, but on how they should be formed in accordance with a human group's values and needs. For Polanyi, as for Aristotle, 'normativity . . . is inseparable from actuality' (*TMEE*, p. 79).

All of this led Polanyi directly to an anthropological approach. The relativistic view of the economy and the concern for the context of values, ethics, and meanings into which economic activity is woven finds clear expression in anthropology. The formalistic or bourgeois attitude of reducing the economy to its essence, choice, is far too restricted for Polanyi's purposes. In anthropology he found a distinctly non-essentialist tradition in which the bias is to let human experience speak for itself through a method grounded in concrete empirical awareness.[12] The anthropological concept of culture, moving ever nearer to a symbolic interactionist frame of reference, is an excellent vehicle to overcome the excessively psychological view of man found in conventional economic theory. Working from a concept of culture, the concern is not for man's essence as a calculative, selfish animal or any other presumed characteristics of human nature, but instead with the interpersonal symbols that control the thought and action of men in any given human group. Although this currently emergent conception of culture in anthropology was not clearly formulated at the time Polanyi turned to the discipline for a reinterpretation of economic theory, it was sufficiently implicit to lead his own work in the symbolic interactionist direction. Of course, the sociology of knowledge interest mentioned above would have led in this direction also.

The political instability that Polanyi experienced directly would have reinforced his conviction that a humane existence in an industrial society could be secured only by a cultural revolution permitting the subordination of economy to human community. His experience with the repression of the Magyar aristocracy and the fascist regimes would have bred not only a fierce democratic commitment but also suggested, confirmed, and fleshed out his ideas about the relation between economy and society. The political instability of capitalist industrial society was experienced with an especially traumatic force in interwar Europe. Moreover, as a refugee from fascism coming to England, Polanyi would have been repeatedly asked about the causes and nature of fascism. In trying to provide an explanation, he and others would have been faced with the problem of freedom versus order in a complex society in a particularly dramatic historical phase. It is not surprising that these were the central topics of discussion in the English planning debate[13] and that Polanyi and Hayek were led to write such similar books in terms of questions asked, notwithstanding the differences in the answers they provided.[14]

The utopian currents in the interwar period, with their passionate visions of a morally regenerated society, may also have influenced Polanyi to some extent. Humphreys goes so far as to attribute to Polanyi's interest in anthropological material the influence of a utopian primitivism or Romanticism, arguing that he was part of a general movement consisting of 'irrational attempts to discover solutions to the economic crisis in the remote past.'[15] I must dissent from Humphreys' view. It is true that Polanyi stressed the moral nature of the institutional crisis of modern capitalism, but it is not clear that to do so warrants the label utopian. Humphreys argues that the call for moral revitalization without a concrete plan of action is utopian, but also makes note of Polanyi's insistence on socialist economic planning. Humphreys cites a review of *The Great Transformation* by Hildebrand,[16] arguing that its author points up the impracticality of the socialist proposal. In fact, however, Hildebrand's criticism is aimed not at the impracticality of planning but at Polanyi's failure to indicate a specific planning model. In any event, one must ask whether it is primitivist and Romanticist to learn from the past. Is it utopian to identify an institutional crisis as a failed moral context? It would be utopian if Polanyi had said care for others because you love them. It is equally utopian or anti-utopian to follow the market ideology that it is irrelevant to care for others. But to search history for institutions that induce caring and cooperation as Polanyi did is not utopian but the height of realism.

I would further disagree with Humphreys' contention that some time in the 1940s Polanyi shifted his attention from democratic industrial society to anthropology because of some conflict between his socialism and his primitivism. Humphreys notes that the discussion of pre-market economies is the least developed section of *The Great Transformation* and that some time between writing it and the late 1940s Polanyi moved into the anthropological study of economic institutions. For Humphreys this shift to anthropological inquiry seems to be a flight from reality on Polanyi's part, born of his inability to blueprint a democratic socialist planning system. However, if socialism is the subordination of economy to human community, how better to learn of it than by studying pre-capitalist economies that were embedded in the total context of the human group? There is also the evident link to the concept of culture already mentioned above. Moreover, if the work on pre-market economies is the least developed section of *The Great Transformation*, and it is, what would be more obvious in the research programme of an individual scholar than to go on and focus attention on that which is least developed at a given point in time? In other words, I see no distinctive shift of emphasis between *The Great Transformation* and Polanyi's later work in anthropology. Instead, I see the development of a well conceived and extraordinarily important research programme.

INFLUENCE

As already noted, Polanyi's principal influence is in anthropology, a field in which there are frequent references to a Polanyi School or Polanyi Group. Indeed, it has been suggested that a paradigm battle is currently in progress in economic anthropology involving the respective research programmes of Polanyi's substantivism, Marxist structuralism, and economic formalism.[17] Polanyi touched off a major methodological controversy with his insistence that formalism was inappropriate to premodern economies. Prior economies in his view were embedded in the total societal fabric in such ways as to make the economy indistinct. Formalism, the logic of economic choice in the face of scarcity, is therefore an inappropriate perspective since it is the expression of a disembedded economy in which individuals explicitly face a wide array of decisions to be made on the basis of explicitly maximizing criteria. The controversy in anthropology is in terms of the applicability to primitive societies of formal economic theory.[18] A closely related issue that is significant to my institutionalist oriented interest in Polanyi is to broaden the compass of the economic theory of advanced industrial societies by treating those societies from the substantive focus. The one controversy thus concerns applying formal economic theory to anthropological studies while the would-be institutionalist controversy involves applying substantive anthropological theory to economic studies. The formalist–substantivist controversy in anthropology thus parallels a much older debate in economics between an approach stressing deductive exploration of individual choice and an alternative approach stressing the empirical, cultural examination of the context in which the economic process unfolds.[19] Polanyi's influence in this regard may have spread into the study of primitive law where, in response to Bohannan's application of Polanyi's themes, a search is underway for substantive categories to be used in comparative legal studies.[20]

Even before the formalist–substantivist controversy, Polanyi's work had spawned a controversy over the economic surplus concept. In the volume that resulted from the Columbia University project in which Polanyi was a guiding force, Harry Pearson criticized the prevalent view of economic development built around the concept of economic surplus (*TMEE*, pp. 320–41). This view theorizes that the level of economic development, taken as the degree to which the economic surplus has expanded beyond subsistence production, is a significant if not all important independent variable in determining the nature of a social economic formation. Pearson argues that this view often commits the same sort of fallacious presumption as the notion that scarcity universally induces economizing actions. Both formulations, that scarcity necessitates choice and that a given level of surplus determines a given degree of development, are fallaciously economistic in Polanyi's sense of bypassing the social cultural context.[21] Society and culture, which for the Polanyi School mediate a human group's objective conditions and its response, human and therefore subjective, are invisible or epiphenomenal in such formulations. Pearson's article engendered a response from Marvin Harris and a brief controversy ensued.[22]

Polanyi has also had some influence on research into the origin and development of trade, money, and markets. His insistence that these elements originated separately and functioned differently in early societies than they do in their unified context in modern societies has stimulated substantial investigation. This is especially true in the areas of primitive money, ports of trade, and spheres of exchange. He insisted that the various functions of money are not necessarily interconnected and may exist independently or with different monetary objects for different functions. In particular, exchange is not prior to or in any way the basis for the other functions of money.[23] Moreover, primitive money is usually special purpose money and not the all purpose money with which the denizens of modern societies are familiar. Ports of trade is Polanyi's term for an economic buffer zone that protects the non-market society from penetration by a commercial society when trade is carried on between the two. This is not only related to Polanyi's work on the position of trade in archaic Greece and his theory of administered trade in general, but also anticipates much of the work done in recent decades on the cultural disruption of premodern economies penetrated by the industrialized countries. Spheres of exchange refers to specialized circulation channels for goods and services of a particular character. For example, there may exist a sphere of prestige goods that do not normally exchange with ordinary goods. Frequently, spheres of exchange operate with special purpose money, i.e. a monetary object that circulates only in exchange for one category of goods and is not translatable into the monetary objects used in other spheres. Polanyi's work on the nature of trade and markets and their place in different societies is highly original and already very influential in anthropology.[24]

Polanyi's concepts of reciprocity and redistribution as alternative means of integrating the division of labour in society are also influential.[25] Reciprocity refers to the circulation of goods and services on the basis of familial or political obligation, reinforced by ritualistic or religious principles. Redistribution is the primarily obligatory delivery of goods and services to a central authority from whence they are reallocated toward public functions, defence, or relief. Such transactions, although often mistaken for market exchanges, are in fact surrounded by very different supporting institutional structures than market exchange and function very differently in the social totality. In particular, in reciprocity and redistribution the flow of economic value is indefinite, often one-sided, and motivated by a variety of cultural contexts. This contrasts sharply with the two-way transfer of equivalent values motivated by self-interested calculation that is characteristic of market exchange. Through these concepts, Polanyi may have indirectly influenced the theory of grants economics that attempts to treat one-way transfers in modern society.[26]

Polanyi has had considerable influence in economic and social history. As in economic anthropology but more so, much of his influence in this regard consists of having posed penetrating and forceful hypotheses that cannot be ignored. His hypotheses have influenced such scholars as Moses Finley in the field of ancient history, A. L. Oppenheim in oriental history, and Douglass North and E. L. Jones in Western economic history.[27] In intellectual history, Polanyi's influence is seen in Joyce Appleby's study of the origin of the market mentality and culture.[28] Polanyi's insistence that the exploitation of labour must be viewed more in terms of cultural disruption than income deprivation alone may have influenced E. P. Thompson and similar social historians, but this is not certain since Polanyi was himself here influenced by Robert Owen and the Hammonds, who may also have influenced these social historians.[29] Finally, the emerging 'political economy' field in sociology is rooted in economic history and displays Polanyi's influence, especially in the works of Immanuel Wallerstein, Terence Hopkins, and Fred Block.[30] In economics Polanyi's influence is less extensive. Although he has had some influence in institutional economics, much of it has either been from those who came directly in contact with him or has come through economic anthropology, which is not surprising given the strong ties in institutional economics to the anthropological perspective.[31] The late Arthur Okun cited

Polanyi's influence in his influential little book on equality and efficiency, and Charles Kindleberger wrote on *The Great Transformation* when asked to contribute to a series of essays on 'Twentieth Century Masterpieces'.[32] Polanyi also influenced Paul Medow's discussion of the humanistic aspects of economic planning.[33] Although Polanyi's influence may be said to be a force toward keeping the Enlightenment tradition alive in economics, it is also true that this influence has not yet been substantial. He remains a relatively neglected economist.

CONCLUSION

From the milieu that has been briefly described emerged Karl Polanyi, very much a figure in the Enlightenment tradition of extending the freedom of individuals to develop their capacities. Freedom for Polanyi was such that it could only be meaningfully exercised by an individual who is existentially responsible, and this responsibility has epistemological, moral, and social aspects.

> By freedom of the spirit we do not mean a denial of truth, nor of ethics, law or authority.
>
> On the contrary, we mean that freedom of the spirit will relentlessly seek truth, abide by the dictates of ethics, act according to the law and respect authority. Relentlessly and consistently. Not calling retreat before any consideration whatsoever, and rousing the human disposition out of its somnolence into ever alert watchfulness. Searching for truth behind and in the face of all and every kind of class-truth and race-truth; following the path of a pure ethic, despite the cut-and-dried precepts of the "moralists", and beyond those; taking its stand on the foundations of justice, even in defiance of the law, and bowing but to the authority of goodness and truth, turning against all phony authority that rests on debauched success and on the display of power. (*LM*, p. xiii)

Freedom is exercised only on a basis of knowledge and understanding; its existence requires a commitment to seek truth. A large part of this truth for Polanyi, indeed his own reality principle, was 'the three constitutive facts in the consciousness of Western man: knowledge of death, knowledge of freedom, knowledge of society'

(*GT*, p. 258a). The individual has a finite life to use and the freedom to use it, but that freedom is not absolute because some degree of conformity and compulsion is necessary to safeguard the survival of the human society without which no human existence or freedom is possible.

Polanyi rejected world views that neglect any of these three constitutive facts. Knowledge of freedom is the necessary context of ethics; knowledge of death and society shape the ethical use of freedom. For Polanyi the freedom to choose and the responsibility for one's choice constitute the essence of ethics. He rejected conventional religious ethics because they contained 'neither moral community nor moral freedom – the twofold basis of every positive ethic'. Hence, the 'trouble with religious ethics is not that it is religious, but that it is not ethical'.[34] Religious ethics, by allowing a choice between a preordained right and wrong but not a choice as to what is right and wrong, drains ethics of its central core of individual moral freedom and responsibility because this core must comprise choices not merely for living by a code but of the code itself. Doctrines that promise everlasting life hide the moral imperative to live well the life one has. Doctrines that hold supernatural forces to be the cause of human action undermine the individual's sense of responsibility for those actions and their consequences. Polanyi also rejected the market mentality because its notion of the individual as responsible only for his own utility function ignores the reality of society. The kind of choices held so important in market culture are also suspect. They constitute frenetic choosing that is but so much coverup for a life devoid of the really important choices. They represent less in the way of living than they do the absence of the commitment to live, i.e. 'endless delay in terms of incessant action'.[35] Polanyi rejected fascism because it denies the reality of freedom in the name of the reality of society, i.e. law and order. He also rejected any utopian scenario that refuses to deal with the social conflict that will not disappear 'come the revolution' because this constitutes a denial of the reality of society. Finally, he rejected the Marxism of the Second International because its historical determinism made society and history into a *deus ex machina* that displaces individual freedom and responsibility.

Society and history *are* important ingredients in the human ethical condition, but in another way, and not simply with respect to the issue of social responsibility *vis-à-vis* law, authority, and the effect of one's actions on others. Society and history are the moral community from which the individual learns about right and wrong. Moral freedom still exists for the individual in choosing a code of what is right and wrong, the proximity of his conduct to that code, and knowledge of his responsibility for these choices and their consequences. In this way Polanyi could accept to a degree the Enlightenment tendency to blame perverse institutions for human shortcomings and the corollary effort to improve institutions and sustain moral progress. But this positive historical thought and action does not relieve the individual of his existential responsibility.

This responsibility entails more than the individual proscribing various transgressions and includes his prescriptions in the use of his life. The individual has a life that matters and the moral imperative to use it well. The reality of death can be grounds for the good life doing good work or for the opposite tendency to nihilism and sloth.

> The revealed reality of death is the ultimate source of the excuses for an empty life. The response of the creative man is to fill that void through work and the permanence of achievement. Hence, art and poetry, science and philosophy, the lone sacrifices of the true soul.[36]

For Polanyi the existential choice is not to live or not, but to live well or not, i.e. not a question of mere existence so much as one of the content and quality of life. His concern was with a Bergsonian *elan vital* and he seems to have accepted Marx's view that consciously and freely undertaken creative activity and creative craft and thought were the essence of the good work that alone can sustain a human existence. This shows clearly in Polanyi's essay on 'Hamlet', in which he anecdotally reveals his own existential dilemma and maturation. In his procrastination Hamlet symbolizes the waste of an uncommitted, non-reflective human life: 'He is unable to decide to live. He can exist only as long as he is not forced to resolve to do so.'[37] Polanyi is making a distinction between mere existence and living, i.e. becoming a developing embodiment of human culture in the rich fabric of human achievement. Polanyi concluded the essay with his view of the underlying appeal and significance of the play.

> "Hamlet" is about the human condition. We all live, insofar as we refuse to die, but we are not resolved to live in all the essential respects in which life invites us. We are postponing happiness, because we hesitate to commit ourselves to live. This is what

> makes Hamlet's delay so symbolic. Life is man's missed opportunity, yet in the end our beloved hero retrieves some of life's fulfillment. The curtain leaves us not only reconciled, but with an unaccountable sense of gratitude towards him, as if his sufferings had not been quite in vain.[38]

Much uncertainty faces the existentially responsible individual in the choices that matter most. Nothing is known absolutely or understood finally about death and salvation or the nature of the good life and the good individual. From such uncertainty freedom grows in the necessity of action and responsibility in a terrain with unknown boundaries. 'The essential uncertainty is the answer to man's existence.'[39] As such, this uncertainty and suffering the *angst* of struggle to make a life worth living in the face of it, is for Polanyi a fact of existence that it is wise to accept.

> Resignation was ever the fount of man's strength and new hope. Man accepted the reality of death and built the meaning of his bodily life upon it. He resigned himself to the truth that he had a soul to lose and that there was worse than death, and founded his freedom upon it. He resigns himself, in our time, to the reality of society which means the end of that freedom. But again, life springs from ultimate resignation. Uncomplaining acceptance of the reality of society gives man indomitable courage and strength to remove all removable injustice and unfreedom. As long as he is true to his task of creating more abundant freedom for all, he need not fear that either power or planning will turn against him and destroy the freedom he is building by their instrumentality. This is the meaning of freedom in a complex society; it gives us all the certainty that we need. (*GT*, p. 258b)

In his life and in his work Polanyi seems to represent a unique and compelling blend of the Enlightenment tradition with the more existential thinking of the twentieth century. His economics was both holistic and sharply focused on the effects of economic forces on the life of the human individual. Indeed, true to the Enlightenment, humanistic tradition, for Polanyi the *raison d'être* of economic study was to more effectively subordinate economic forces to the fundamental purpose of individual freedom and development. He sought to correct the dominant economic ideology of our times with its peculiar illusion that a rat race of pecuniary self-aggrandizement serves this purpose.

> The understanding of power and material values deprives us of an illusory freedom and re-creates it in terms of reality, as an existence that fills the universe as we know it does, not stopping other lives or taking away their meanings. Analysis of our function of creating material power and value is also the true analysis of our capacity to create freedom.[40]

The term *lives and livelihood* expresses Polanyi's method and implies his conviction. His method, that of social or institutional economics, is to study the economy as it is is placed in society, i.e. the ways in which economic activity is instituted and the ways in which that institutedness affects society, polity, and culture. Polanyi's conviction was that the good economy is one that provisions the lives of individuals, provides for their fullest development, and does so without disrupting or distorting those lives or their development. His motive for studying the place of economy in society was to induce people to put the economy in its place and keep it there. He thought and felt, and I wholeheartedly agree, that this is the central problem of existence and the most imperative struggle of our times.

2 The Methodology of Economics

Polanyi's work, broadly speaking, can be said to have been motivated by two basic concerns, one of which was concerned with the general problem of methodology and the other with a historical problem of political economy. Polanyi's work was part of a wider movement once referred to as economic sociology. As Harry Pearson noted,

> The impetus for the widely current efforts in the direction of an economic sociology comes from the increasing array of empirical problems met by all social scientists who must face up to economies as social systems. The problems arise in two different areas of interest; those involving premarket economies, both literate and nonliterate, and those where contemporary departures from the pattern of a self-regulating system of markets pose the problem. Attempts to deal systematically with these distinctly separate empirical problems converge on a common interest: the establishment of a generally relevant theory of economic organization and development. (*TMEE*, p. 307)

The methodological problem centred on the relations among economic anthropology, economic history, comparative economic systems, and the scope of economic theory in general. The historical problem of political economy was concerned with the breakdown of the international political economic system early in this century and the subsequent development of the corporate–welfare state. These two concerns are interrelated. The methodological animus may indeed be considered subordinate to the problem of political economy because Polanyi was dedicated to the proposition that 'history should be made to yield answers to some of the burning moral and operational problems of our own age' (*LM*, p. xxxix). The new economic theory which Polanyi expected to emerge from his methodological discussion was seen by him as necessary to comprehend the logic of the political economy of market capitalism. This comprehension in turn would enable democratic society to break through the impasse created by industrialism as instituted via market capitalism. In this chapter and Chapter 3, I elaborate Polanyi's approach to economic analysis. In Chapter 4, this discussion will be applied to Polanyi's political economic concern, the nature and evolution of market capitalism. With this, the way will have been made for considering the substantive and most pressing problem, the nature and crisis of the corporate–welfare state and the means by which the Gordian knot of the contemporary institutional impasse can be cut through.

ECONOMIC ANTHROPOLOGY AND COMPARATIVE ECONOMIC SYSTEMS

Polanyi's methodological animus stemmed from his recognition of the essential theoretical affinity between economic anthropology and comparative economic systems. Theory is important to any social science but the nature of anthropology adds to its significance, as George Dalton points out:

> One of the peculiarities of economic anthropology is that neither the facts nor the folk views of primitive economic life are in doubt. The ethnographic record is large and detailed. What is in doubt is the most useful theoretical approach to organize the many descriptive accounts . . . (*PAME*, p. xxxviii)

A theory of economic anthropology is possible only if the research programme on primitive and archaic social economies is viewed as being a part of comparative economic systems. The categories important to the modern social economy have their counterparts in earlier societies. Quoting Dalton again:

> In order for anthropologists to see what is analytically important in Trobriands' economy they must first understand the structure of industrial capitalism; to understand the special usage of pig-tusk and cowrie money, they must first understand the organization and usage of dollars and francs. (*PAME*, p. x)

The differentiating characteristics of a socioeconomic system emerge only through comparative analysis which makes possible the specification of a given system's peculiarities as opposed to those dimensions which it shares with other socioeconomic formations.

Although this is true of the organizational comparison of the economic systems of a given epoch, which therefore have much in common, it is more forcefully true in the consideration of social evolution. The capitalism of America and Europe, and even the socialisms of the Soviet bloc, have much in common with one another because they are all modern, industrial economies with similar concerns and problems of efficiency, growth, urbanization, and social psychology. Comparative analysis one with the others nonetheless reveals critical historical and organizational differences, and the danger of succumbing to the methodological trap of ethnocentrism and neglect of cultural relativity is considerable. These differences and the concomitant methodological issues pale before their counterparts in the study of primitive and archaic social economies. In this instance it is even more important to avoid the neglect of the cultural context which surrounds and motivates the production and distribution of goods and services.

At the same time, the very factors which promote or allow such ethnocentrism establish the importance of comparative historical analysis. All economies, that is all the material spheres of human societies, involve the provisioning of human purposes by the technological interaction with, and transformation of, nature. In all but the most primitive societies, there is also division of labour with the concomitant necessity of integrative institutions to coordinate economic activities. These institutions have at least superficial similarities – market-places, trade, monetary objects, and accounting devices (see *PAME*, pp. xli–xlii). The presence of these categorical generalities simultaneously makes it fruitful to undertake transcultural comparisons and establishes the need for methodological discipline so that fundamental and instructive differences are not swept under the rug of hasty generalizations and ethnocentrism. There is much to be learned from comparison of primitive and modern social economies *if* oversimplification and neglect of concrete cultural contexts is avoided. Marx had earlier offered this very caution.

> Bourgeois society is the most developed and the most complex historic organization of production. The categories which express its relations, the comprehension of its structure, thereby also allow insights into the structure and the relations of production of

> all the vanished social formations out of whose ruins and elements it built itself up, whose partly still unconquered remnants are carried along within it, whose mere nuances have developed explicit significance within it, etc. Human anatomy contains a key to the anatomy of the ape. The intimations of higher development among the subordinate animal species, however, can be understood only after the higher development is already known. The bourgeois economy thus supplies the key to the ancient, etc. But not at all in the manner of those economists who smudge over all historical differences and see bourgeois relations in all forms of society. One can understand tribute, tithe, etc., if one is acquainted with ground rent. But one must not identify them.[1]

In addition to the need for totality and cultural context, another instructive lesson to be learned from these categorical similarities is the need for a process or evolutionary focus. Socioeconomic categories have life-processes of origin, maturity, and decline. If it be true, as MacIver credited Aristotle (*GT*, p. ix), that 'we can learn the nature of anything only when it has reached – and – passed – its maturation', it is no less true that one can learn about the mature category by the conditions of its origin and development. The analogy to the relation of childhood environment to the adult human being, and vice versa, seems to be entirely apt. Institutions have their origin and a period of dependence, in which they are peripheral to the predominant institutions of the historical period. In the process of social evolution, institutions develop and may reach a period of maturity in which they are the predominant and typifying characteristics of the historical period. They then age and reach their period of senility and decline, begging their replacement by newly maturing institutions. For example, wage-labour and capital existed for centuries in the periphery of societies organized along different principles. In capitalism, wage-labour and capital emerge in their mature, historically significant form as the dominant socioeconomic categories. In their senescence, wage-labour and capital will be replaced by the categories which are typical and predominant in a new post-capitalist social order. Polanyi's principal example was the market institution: 'though . . . fairly common since the later Stone Age, its role was no more than incidental to economic life' (*GT*, p. 43). The prominent historian, Lynn White, Jr, has made a similar point with respect to feudalism.

> [In the eighth century] the ancient custom of swearing allegiance to a leader (vassalage) was fused with the granting of an estate (benefice), and the result was feudalism.
>
> [Opponents of this theory of the origin of feudalism insist] that the union of benefice and vassalage is far older than the eighth century ... [Proponents of the theory counter that] "whether the military benefice was or was not an eighth century invention is a matter of secondary importance. Our chief interest is rather the wide extension of feudal tenure [in the eighth century]." [The] approximation of feudal relationships before the Carolingian era [are best thought of as] "proto-feudal" ...
>
> The historical record is replete with inventions [and relationships] which have remained dormant in a society until at last . . . they "awaken" and become active elements in the shaping of a culture to which they are not entirely novel.[2]

The point is that the methodology of economic anthropology should contain or be part of comparative economic analysis. As Dalton observes,

> a theory of economic anthropology becomes possible only when primitive and archaic economies are regarded as part of comparative economic systems. To understand what is special to the economies anthropologists deal with and what they share with all other economies requires comparative analysis of the kind Polanyi provides. In order for anthropologists to see what is analytically important in Trobriands' economy they must first understand the structure of industrial capitalism; to understand the special usage of pig-tusk and cowrie money, they must first understand the organization and usage of dollars and francs. One reason why theory in economic anthropology remains underdeveloped is that anthropologists have not brought to the economic branch of their subject the same comparative grounding they bring to kinship, law, politics, and religion. (*PAME*, p. x)

Polanyi's concern was a knife edge cutting both ways. He saw not only the need to treat economic anthropology as a component of comparative economic systems but also the importance of economic anthropology to comparative economic systems. Specifically, he found a vital defect in the methodology of comparative economic systems which could be corrected only by the incorporation of the insights of economic anthropology into comparative economic analysis. Comparative economic systems is primarily and excessively concerned with organizational comparisons of modern industrial economies. These comparisons are made in terms of the formal, economizing models of a market economy. This approach is to a considerable extent inaccurate on its own turf: although industrialized economies share common traits of concern for rationality, efficiency, stability, and growth, they also display important differences due to their cultural heritage and many facets and problems of economic behaviour are invisible to the economistic purview. Polanyi sought to overcome this limited vision by 'the linking up of economic history with social anthropology' (*GT*, p. 45). The economic history of precapitalist economies is then a vital area for the comparison of economic systems. The neglect of the historical dimension and the cultural totality of human behaviour is a recognized limitation of the formal, organization approach. In other words, Dalton's,

> The historians concerned with pre-industrial economies and the economists concerned with comparative economic systems have much to learn from economic anthropology. Firsthand accounts of primitive economy are as close to a laboratory as economic historians and those concerned with comparative economy can get.
>
> This should not come as a surprise. The economic historians today are teaching us about African and Asian economic development by pointing out what was special to European and American development. So, too, can we learn about modern communistic and welfare state economies by contrasting them with the pre-industrial systems we call primitive, peasant, and archaic. Polanyi's work provides a corrective to one of the shortcomings in the field of comparative economic systems: its almost exclusive concern with recent and contemporary industrial economies. The field is too narrowly confined to comparisons of industrial capitalism ... and industrial communism. The areas of fruitful comparison can be widened. The specialized subjects that are economic anthropology and economic history should be treated as part of comparative economy. (*PAME*, p. xi)

When the scope of transcultural comparative analysis is historical rather than simply spatial, the limitation of the economizing viewpoint becomes a fatal defect. Indeed, as Dalton has quoted

Melville Herskovits, the 'attention of economists has been focused . . . on just those aspects of our economy least likely to be found' in primitive economies of interest to the anthropologist (*PAME*, p. xl). The prevalent notion as to the ubiquity of calculative, gain-oriented economic behaviour is especially important in this regard.

> The institutional structure of the economy need not compel, as with the market system, economizing actions. The implications of such an insight for all the social sciences which must deal with the economy could hardly be more far-reaching. Nothing less than a fundamentally different starting point for the analysis of the human economy as a social process is required. (*PAME*, p. 118)

The pursuit of gain through exchange is an institutionally enforced pattern of behaviour which must be analysed as a result rather than as the antecedent of the historical process. Once again, Marx put the matter well in his criticism of classical political economy.

> Smith and Ricardo . . . [follow] the eighteenth-century prophets, in whose imaginations this eighteenth-century individual [of the society of free competition] – the product on one side of the dissolution of feudal forms of society, on the other side of the new forces of production developed since the sixteenth century – appears as an ideal whose existence they project into the past. Not as a historic result but as history's point of departure. As the Natural Individual appropriate to their notion of human nature, not arising historically, but posited by nature.[3]

Obviously, Marx was objecting to the use of natural law philosophy to support the contention that market capitalism is inevitably and transhistorically the social formation most consistent with invariant human nature – Smith's 'natural propensity to truck, barter, and exchange' in the pursuit of economic gain. As I shall return to below, even without an explicit natural law framework, modern economists carry on this fundamentally conservative inference that the human individual is naturally calculative and in pursuit of economic gain. This institutional fixation is precisely the paralytic quality expressed by Polanyi's term, *market mentality*, and it was this blighted vision which vested Polanyi's interest in methodology with its political economic urgency. Polanyi foresaw that this narrowness of economic theory could be overcome only by the availability of a wider empirical basis for economic theory, and that the integration of economic anthropology, economic history, and comparative economic systems into a comprehensive universal or general economic history was the way to achieve this wider basis.

THE TWO MEANINGS OF ECONOMIC

In order to develop these methodological concerns, and free the construction of a universal economic history from the formalist bias of conventional economic theory, Polanyi developed and frequently used a distinction between two meanings of the root term *economic*. He referred to these as the *formal* and *substantive* meanings of economic.

> The formal meaning ... stemming from the means-end relationship ... is a universal whose referents are not restricted to any one field of human interest. Logical or mathematical terms of this sort are called *formal* in contrast to the specific areas to which they are applied. Such a meaning underlies the verb *maximizing*, more popularly, economizing ... (*LM*, p. 20)

The one connotation, formalism, is used almost exclusively by mainstream economists. Its key hallmark is that of gain-oriented, maximizing choice; i.e. the formal connotation embodies the notion of calculative, economizing behaviour. Faced with the ineluctable fact of scarcity, human societies also confront the inevitable necessity of choosing. Any society and, indeed, especially its constituent individuals, must by one means or another make priority decisions on the allocation and distribution of productive capacity. Coupled with the further postulate or ideal typology of rationality, economics becomes the *science of choice*, and its typical concern is the deductive exploration of the logic of maximizing under the constraint of scarcity. The classic statement is still that of Lionel, Lord Robbins, and I shall often employ quotations from his pivotal consideration of the scope and method of economic science in the discussion that follows.

Coupled with the liberal ethos of individualism, this formalist framework virtually eclipses the traditional social setting of economic activity. The liberal values of individual self-reliance, initiative, self-sovereignty, and personal development take on an untoward narrowness; self-gain is the celebrated motive, freedom is the liberty to make a buck, and personal growth is the accumulation of wealth. Indeed, society becomes but the aggregate of the decisions made by 'economic man' with given preferences and capacities in the face of market situations. No important conception emerges from the formalist perspective of social value as anything more than the sum of private values.[4] Despite some ebb and flow, the formalist bent has been the predominant focus of mainstream economics in the twentieth century, especially in the post-World War II period in which a veritable formalist revolution was sustained. The formalist perspective is a-historical and, in addition to the narrowness of its psychological and empirical reach, it embodies a fatal defect in its neglect of social change. This defect, as I have argued elsewhere, is the really tragic legacy of mainstream economics.[5]

Polanyi countered this economistic conception with the substantive connotation of economic as material. The substantive connotation centres on the necessity that humanity, in order to get its living, must interact with the rest of nature. The substantive connotation refers to the material function of the economy. The latter means no more, no less than the nature-imposed necessity that all its species must get a living for themselves. One of Polanyi's titles, *The Livelihood of Man*, is central to his conception of economic. The substantive meaning stems, in brief, from man's patent dependence for his livelihood upon nature and his fellows. He survives by virtue of an institutionalized interaction between himself and his natural surroundings. That process is the economy, which supplies him with the means of satisfying his material wants (*LM*, p. 20).

The reference to 'material wants' is not to be interpreted as a naturalistic conception of human wants. Polanyi, with some semantic difficulties, was quick to deflect any possible misunderstanding in this regard.

> This phrase [i.e., material wants] should not be taken to signify that the wants to be satisfied are exclusively bodily needs, such as food and shelter, however essential these be for his [man's] survival, for such a restriction would absurdly restrict the realm of the economy. The means, not the wants, are material. Whether the useful objects are required to avert starvation or are needed for educational, military, or religious purposes is irrelevant. So long as the wants depend for their fulfillment on material objects, the reference is economic. Economic here denotes nothing else

> than "bearing reference to the process of satisfying material wants." To study human livelihood is to study the economy in this substantive sense of the term. . . . (*LM*, p. 20)

Human purposes are not materialistic, but the means of their achievement frequently are, and it is the materiality of means that typifies the economic facet of human life. Elsewhere, Polanyi recognized the danger of allowing the study of man's livelihood to drift toward the naturalistic conception. 'All strivings for . . . a naturalistic economics remained unsuccessful. . . . No mere naturalistic concept of the economy can . . . compete' with the formalist analysis of a market economy (*PAME*, p. 118). The substantive conception, if it is to hold its own in the paradigm battle with formalism, must not degenerate to mere naturalism. In an earlier statement, Polanyi avoided this semantic problem by referring to 'want-satisfying material means' (*PAME*, p. 145) rather than material wants.

Not surprisingly, the two connotations of the root term *economic* provide the basis for two different definitions of the economic system and two perspectives from which to approach economic analysis. The formal approach to defining economic systems turns, of course, on the axiomatic basis of scarcity, rationality, and choice. This axiomatic basis appears

> to establish the range of the formal meaning as comprising the economy in all its manifestations. For the economy, however instituted, would then consist of scarce means under conditions that induce acts of choice among the different uses of the insufficient means, and, consequently, be capable of description in the formal terms of the scarcity definition. (*LM*, p. 25)

> [E]conomizing action, the essence of rationality, is, then, regarded as a manner of disposing of time and energy so that a maximum of goals are achieved out of this man–nature relationship. And the economy becomes the locus of such action. (*PAME*, p. 117)

The formal meaning then 'denotes the economy as a sequence of acts of economizing, i.e. of choices induced by scarcity situations' (*PAME*, p. 145). Statements to this effect abound in conventional economics textbooks. The economy is less a matter of work, production, technology, products, and consumption than it is a matter of choosing. Not classes of workers, capitalists, and *rentier*, engaged in economic activity in a variety of ways and with diverse motives, populate the economic system, but instead the economy is peopled by amorphous decision-makers singularly intent upon maximum gain.

Polanyi sharply dissented from this reduction of the economic system to a process of sentient choice with its own internal logic. He argued that 'we must rid ourselves of the ingrained notion that the economy is a field of experience of which human beings have necessarily always been conscious' (*PAME*, p. 119). The economic function, material provisioning, has, of course, always been present, but it does not necessarily follow that societies have a conception of a distinct subsystem, the economy, with its own distinct logic and governing principles. In other words, the substantive economy is universal, the calculative economy is not. This much is clear from Polanyi's insistence that the vital typological condition for the substantive economy is that 'so long as the wants depend for their fulfillment on material objects, the reference is economic'. Emphatically, the relation between the wants and the material objects need not involve choice in the formal sense. Neither scarcity nor maximization are crucial to the substantive conception of the economy.

Not choice but livelihood or provisioning is the vision underlying the substantivist definition of the economic system. This vision is expressed in Aristotle's 'concept of the economy [as] an institutionalized process through which sustenance is secured' (*LM*, p. 30); it is from this point of departure that Polanyi develops the concept of the substantive economy.

> The economy as an instituted process of interaction serving the satisfaction of material wants forms a vital part of every human community. Without an economy in this sense, no society could exist for any length of time.
>
> The substantive economy must be understood as being constituted on two levels: one is the interaction between man and his surroundings; the other is the institutionalization of that process. (*LM*, p. 31)

In other words, the economy involves two sets of interaction. Nature imposes upon mankind the necessity of interacting with his natural environment in order to sustain his livelihood. For one man, the isolated Robinson Crusoe, the economy would be reduced to this level. Crusoe would have to have some knowledge of his island's ecology in order to carry out his economic activity. This engineering competency would complete his field of referents for guiding his economy. In a true social economy, however, the individual's ecological judgment is not sufficient per se. It is also necessary that the individual have a working knowledge of other participants in the social economy.[6] This is the social problem of integration or institutedness of economic behaviour. As Adolph Lowe observes, it is essentially a system of communication and sanction. The individual needs to be informed of what is expected of him in certain situations, and what he can expect of others. He also needs to know what sanctions exist and will be applied to ensure expected behaviour. This system of communication and sanction, spanning the spectrum from personal moral responsibility to social accountability, is the institutedness of the substantive economy. The economic system, or the economic function of social activity, is therefore a more or less systematic and orderly pattern of social behaviour which functions to provision the material wherewithal necessary to support social and individual life. The materiality conception of the economy refers to the *instituted process* by which society provisions itself, and this connotation emphasizes technology, change, and society, and the comparison of the institutional patterns of different economies. The market economy and its institutions of calculative behaviour and the search for personal advantage through exchange is one such pattern, but only one such. Moreover, even at this, the predominance of calculativeness over caprice, habit, and empathy in the market economy is sufficiently lax to delimit the economistic conception in some regards. At any rate, calculative behaviour is not spontaneous; it must be instituted through acculturation in the same way as any other social trait.

Obviously, two such very different visions of the economic system must lead to two very different approaches to economic theory. Once again, Lord Robbins is as good a weather vane as any for contrasting the formalist view to that of Polanyi. Robbins argues that four conditions must be met if a phenomenal situation is to provide a problem for economic science. There must be various ends or goals, limited means for achieving these ends, these ends must be capable of alternative applications, and the ends must be of varying importance.[7] Moreover, for Robbins, if these conditions are met, 'then behaviour necessarily assumes the form of choice'. Hence economic science may not be concerned with given productive and consumptive activities at all if the activities do not meet these conditions. Conversely, any activities which do meet these conditions provide scientific problems for economics whether or not the activities are generally conceived as economic. Robbins' conception of economic science

> focuses attention on a particular *aspect* of behaviour, the form imposed by the influence of scarcity. It follows from this, therefore, that in so far as it presents this aspect, any kind of human behaviour falls within the scope of economic generalizations. We do not say that the production of potatoes is economic activity and the production of philosophy is not. We say rather that, in so far as either kind of activity involves the relinquishment of other desired alternatives, it has its economic aspect. There are no limitations on the subject-matter of Economic Science save this.[8]

Apparently, the contemporary extension of the choice framework to the selection of spouses, procreation, etc. would brook no demurrer from Lord Robbins.

The substantivist approach to economic theory is black where the formalist approach is white. The substantivist conceives of the economy 'as *a component of culture* rather than *a kind of human action*, the material life process of society rather than a need-satisfying process of individual behavior'.[9] Polanyi insists that economic theory must include non-calculative motivations and material activity whether or not scarcity exists or is believed to exist. Thus, whereas Robbins excludes non-choice situations involving material means from economic consideration, the substantivist view insists that material means are the prime concern of economic analysis. In a passage in which Polanyi laments that, although there have been many substantivist economists, they have been brushed aside by the predominance of the formalist bent, he also elaborates the contrast between the two approaches.

> These thinkers emphasized the substantive meaning of *economic*. They identified the economy with industry rather than business; with technology rather than ceremonialism; with means of production rather than titles to property; with capital goods rather than capital – in short, with the economic substance rather than its marketing form and terminology. (*LM*, p. 6)

The reference to 'marketing form' signifies the heavy ideological overtones surrounding the two approaches. Although I know of no apparent logical reason, the historical record of controversy clearly shows an ideological cleavage running roughly parallel to the two approaches to economics. The substantivist approach, notably in its outcroppings in German Historicism, Marxism and American Institutionalism, tends to have its ranks filled with scholars with a leftward inclination in social philosophy. The opposite inclination, and perhaps the centrist one, is the tendency of those holding to the formalist perspective. This clustering is not wholly inexplicable despite its lack of logical necessity. The choice framework focuses on the relations of given means to given ends in an atmosphere of individual maximization. The market categories here take on an air of inevitability, invariance, and immutability. The categories of power, socioeconomic class, and social change are singularly absent in the formalist schema. The substantivist view tends to afford far more attention to historical experience and social change. To suggest that matters were once different is to suggest that they could be different again, and this serves to refute any immutability of institutional arrangements. At any rate, the substantivists generally subscribe to far more in the way of political control of economic activity than their formalist colleagues.[10]

Despite this tendency for ideological clustering at the two poles of meaning, there would appear to be no logical invalidation of an eclectic coexistence between the two.[11] There are, after all, exceptions to the rule, formalists who are leftists and historicists who are rightists. Polanyi himself saw no necessary wrongheadedness in employing economic as a compound of the two meanings, notwithstanding the heavy emphasis he put on distinguishing them. He argued that the two meanings have 'separate roots', 'entirely different origins', and 'nothing in common' (*LM*, pp. 19–20). Elsewhere,

> the formal meaning of *economic* bears in fact only an accidental reference to the substantive meaning. The "material" character of the want satisfaction is given whether there is maximizing or not; and maximizing is given whether the means and ends are material or not. (*LM*, pp. 26–7)

Nonetheless, Polanyi did not object to using the compound conception of economic which embodies both the formal and substantive senses – not, that is, if certain precautions are observed. These precautions must be taken so that the two meanings are not 'naively compounded'.

> Such a merger of meanings is, of course, unexceptionable as long as we remain conscious of its restrictive effects. But the current concept of economic fuses the "subsistence" and the "scarcity" meanings of economic without a sufficient awareness of the dangers to clear thinking inherent in that merger. (*PAME*, pp. 140–1)

Polanyi's caveat is important; he did not insist upon keeping the two meanings distinct merely to engage in ideological polemics nor to deny the appropriateness of eclecticism in some situations. His purpose was instead to counter the 'market mentality' which permeates the formalist approach. I have touched upon this mentality as *ethnocentrism* in the approach to the comparison of economic systems. In the context of general economic theory, this mentality is termed the 'economistic fallacy'. This fallacy was the threat to clarity of thought that Polanyi saw in the naive compounding of the two meanings.

> The economistic fallacy ... consists in a tendency to equate the human economy with its market form. Accordingly, to eliminate this bias, a radical clarification of the meaning of the word *economic* is required. Again, this cannot be achieved unless all ambiguity is removed and the formal and the substantive meanings are separately established. (*LM*, p. 20)

The fallacy persists amidst the confusion, and clarification is required to dispel it.

The economistic fallacy is crucial to the task of this book, and I consider it in detail in the next section. To cap the present section, it is only necessary to add that Lord Robbins is no less emphatic than Polanyi in his separation of the two meanings. Robbins chastises the economists of the English tradition for their persistent use of 'concern with material welfare' as the hallmark of economic analysis. He finds this a curious and confusing offence given 'the unanimity with which they [the English economists] have adopted a non-material definition of "productivity" '.[12] No doubt Lord Robbins would like to see what he might refer to as the materialist or institutionalist fallacy removed from economic science by the same clarification that Polanyi invoked. No matter what is one's persuasion in the ongoing *methodenstreit*, Lord Robbins deserves considerable gratitude for the honesty and clarity with which he broached the methodological problem. Without his cogent elucidation, the task ahead would most certainly be much more difficult.

THE ECONOMISTIC FALLACY

The economistic fallacy consists of 'an artificial indentification of the economy with its market form' (*PAME*, p. 142n). The problem is not limited to economists as indicated by Harry Pearson in his review of a book by two eminent sociologists, Talcott Parsons and Neil Smelser:

> By thus joining a formal category of action, economizing, with an empirical entity, the economy, the authors have committed a fateful error. Inevitably, the economy tends to be identified with its market form. The source of the error appears to be in their having confused the functional requirement of adaptation to environment in the process of achieving system goals with one of the modes of adaptation, namely, economizing. (*TMEE*, p. 313; italics omitted)

Patently and radically ethnocentric, the economistic *gestalt* raises the habits and motives of a particular historical period and its specific institutional configuration to the status of universal, generic categories. Polanyi chose the word fallacy with care; for him, economism constitutes a logical error. The error is

> in equating the human economy in general with its market form. . . . The fallacy itself is patent: the physical aspect of man's needs is part of the human condition; no society can exist that does not possess some kind of substantive economy. The supply-demand-price mechanism, on the other hand . . ., is a comparatively modern institution of specific structure. . . . To narrow the sphere of the genus *economic* specifically to market phenomena is to eliminate the greatest part of man's history from the scene. On the other hand, to stretch the concept of the market until it embraces all economic phenomena is artificially to invest all things

> economic with the peculiar characteristics that accompany the phenomenon of the market. Inevitably, clarity of thought is impaired. (*LM*, p. 6)

The economistic fallacy commits the logical error of misplaced concreteness. Alfred North Whitehead defined the *fallacy of misplaced concreteness* as 'identifying abstract conceptions with reality',[13] or again, as 'neglecting the degree of abstraction involved when an actual entity is considered merely so far as it exemplifies certain categories of thought'.[14] It is precisely Polanyi's point that the economistic fallacy identifies an abstract model with reality, and especially that it considers empirical economic behaviour only insofar as that behaviour corresponds to the postulates of the formal, maximizing model. This is very nearly what Schumpeter had in mind in his concept of the *Ricardian vice*, i.e. jumping to policy conclusions from a highly abstract, almost tautological basis.[15] It is quite possible that Ricardo's disservice to the profession in this respect outweighs his positive contribution in other respects.

> It is very arguable that the science of political economy as studied in its first period after the death of Adam Smith (1790), did more harm than good. It destroyed many economic fallacies. . . . But it riveted on men a certain set of abstractions which were disastrous in their influence on modern mentality. It dehumanized industry . . . and fix[ed] attention on a definite group of abstractions, neglected[ed] everything else, and elicit[ed] every scrap of information and theory which [was] relevant to what it . . . retained.[16]

Similarly, T. W. Hutchison dissents from the view that the intellectual gains of the 'Ricardian methodological revolution' outweigh its 'very serious intellectual losses'.[17] At any rate, despite the discarding of much of Ricardo's theoretical system, modern economics certainly retains the Ricardian vice and fallacy of misplaced concreteness. 'It is beyond dispute . . . that the sin of standard economics is the fallacy of misplaced concreteness . . .'.[18] Modern economics is methodologically quite different from Adam Smith in its formalism, which is the legacy of Ricardo. As J. M. Buchanan has observed:

> Smith did not . . . seek to accomplish his didactic purpose by

> elaborating his theoretical model. Instead he applied the analysis . . . to the actual economy. . . . The starting point remained always the institutions that he observed. . . . Modern economic theorists proceed quite differently. They analyze abstract and formal models which may bear little or no relationship to the institutions that may exist.[19]

The economistic fallacy is also an error of logic in the sense that its conclusion is inconsistent with the facts of social evolution.

As the quotation from Buchanan suggests, the pernicious legacy of economistic thinking is seen most clearly in its eclipse of institutional analysis. Institutional analysis consists of 'those conceptual tools required to penetrate the maze of social relationships in which the economy' has been implanted (*PAME*, p. 120). The concern of institutional analysis is the systematic, comparative study of those social arrangements and habits of mind by which human society institutes its economic function, i.e. by which it vests economic activity with meaning and stability. In other words, Allen Sievers's institutional analysis is 'concerned with the social institutions by means of which economic functions are performed'.[20] In Polanyi's view, the tool kit of concepts for institutional analysis had yet to be established. I consider the institutional concepts that Polanyi developed in the next chapter, but such concepts cannot in any event be brought to fruition without the penetration and transcendence of the economistic fallacy.

Economism preempts institutional analysis by presupposing the psychology of economic activity and prefiguring the nature and task of economic institutions. Under economism, 'the economy *however instituted*, . . . consist[s] of scarce means under conditions that induce acts of choice' (*LM*, p. 25; emphasis added). To see that the eclipse of institutional analysis is not mere fanciful conjecture, it is only necessary to invoke once again the authority of Lord Robbins.

> But it is one thing to contend that economic analysis has *most interest and utility* in an exchange economy. It is another to contend that its subject-matter is *limited* to such phenomena. . . . [I]t is clear that behaviour outside the exchange economy is conditioned by the same limitation of means in relation to ends as behaviour within the economy, and is capable of being subsumed under the same fundamental categories. The generalizations of the theory of value are as applicable to the behaviour of isolated

> man or the executive authority of a communist society, as to the behaviour of man in an exchange economy – even if they are not so illuminating in such contexts. The exchange relationship is a *technical* incident, . . . subsidiary to the main fact of scarcity.[21]

It is scarcely necessary to add that 'scarcity of means to satisfy ends of varying importance is an almost ubiquitous condition of human behaviour'.[22] For economic analysis of the economistic ilk, there is no call to delve into the concrete aspirations, powers, and foibles of the lives of given people. Economic analysis knows a priori what it needs to know about their lives; it knows in advance what constitutes their economic problem. In effect, economic analysis need not know the people whose economic activities it is bent on studying.

This ethnocentric eclipse of institutional analysis has serious consequences for social science and philosophy. It virtually guarantees that the *actual* needs, wants, motives, and interests of any given people will not be ferreted out, described, and analysed – unless, of course, the concrete human situation happens to match those postulated by the formalist perspective. The situation from which the formalist postulates developed – to the extent they had any basis outside of logic – was the competitive period of market capitalism, a very narrow historical era, indeed. On the broad historical record the motive of gain and the calculative categories are neither always present nor are they often predominant even when they are present (*GT*, p. 47). Yet the formalist approach, with its Achilles heel of the economistic fallacy, universalizes the gain motive.

> The semblance is compelling that hunger and gain are *the* incentives on which any economic system must rest. This assumption is baseless. Ranging over human societies, we find hunger and gain not appealed to as incentives to production, and where so appealed to, they are fused with other powerful motives. (*PAME*, pp. 64–5)

It is wrong on the face of it to promote hunger and gain as *the* economic motives. Indeed, they are no more economic than other motives, and this too is part of the economistic fallacy. 'This new world of "economic motives" was based on a fallacy. Intrinsically, hunger and gain are no more "economic" than love or hate, pride or prejudice. No human motive is per se economic' (*PAME*, p. 63). Of course, this is not to deny the ontological necessity of food provisioning. The point is only that hunger per se need not provide the psychological impetus to food provisioning.

> Assuredly, if we do not eat, we must perish. . . . But the pangs of hunger are not automatically translated into an incentive to produce. Production is not an individual, but a collective affair. If an individual is hungry, there is nothing definite for him to do. . . . With man, the political animal, everything is given not by natural, but by social circumstance. What made the nineteenth century think of hunger and gain as "economic" was simply the organization of production under a market economy.
>
> Hunger and gain are here linked with production through the need of "earning an income." For under such a system, man, if he is to keep alive, is compelled to buy goods on the market with the help of an income derived from selling other goods on the market. (*PAME*, p. 64)

In others words, food must be provided, but how it is provided is a matter of how the productive and distributive function is *instituted*. The individual may be socialized to sell and buy to satisfy his hunger, but he may instead be taught by society to petition a political figure or depend upon a relative for it.

If, though, the social theorist *assumes* economic activity to be gain-oriented, then gain must *appear* to be the motive back of the productive and distributive function. This is the fallacy of misplaced concreteness in the formalist context. Under its thrall, primitive and archaic economies must be viewed as quasi-market economies and such actual motivations as reciprocal gift-giving or customary tithe-offering are then mistakenly rendered as exchange-for-gain activities (*PAME*, pp. 120–2). Hence, as K. William Kapp has observed, 'The mainstream of economic analysis still avoids placing man, with his actual needs and requirements, in the center of its theoretical considerations.'[23]

The problem is not merely the methodology of economic history and anthropology. To the extent that modern economic behaviour is performed under non-gain impetuses, or a mixture of gain and non-gain motives, the economistic fallacy provides incorrect or incomplete guidance to economic policy. One of the themes of Adolph Lowe's important book, *On Economic Knowledge*, already cited above, is that contemporary economic policy is hampered by the unrealistic behavioural assumptions of mainstream economic analysis. Specifically, Lowe argues that the extremum, or maximization, principle which orthodoxy assumes and which corresponded well to early competitive capitalism, is no longer enforced by socioeconomic conditions. Policy based on the assumption that the extremum principle is operative is therefore misguided. In an earlier book, Lowe gave a more specific example, that of the so-called *Rentenmark* in Germany in 1923.[24] The treasury, desperately seeking to control inflation, pressed ahead with a policy that the best economic minds were convinced would fail and, indeed, make matters worse. The policy was successful! The key to the success was an appeal to patriotism and solidarity, psychological ingredients that economists were not equipped to include in their deliberations because of their assumption that people would respond to the policy initiative along the lines of the extremum principle.

The economistic fallacy also obscures important considerations by its presumption of scarcity. The formalist perspective leaves no room to consider empirically whether or not an insufficiency of means exists, or whether or not insatiability does in fact characterize the material appetites of given people at a given time and place. The substantivist perspective does, of course, leave open the questions of scarcity and insatiability. Indeed, as Aristotle emphasized, the substantivist orientation must reject insatiability in absolute terms because nothing in nature is boundless (*LM*, p. 30). The scarcity and insatiability prejudice is important. Lowe observes that 'the notion of unconditional scarcity turns a deaf ear to the promise of this revolt – the eventual . . . conquest of the stinginess of nature'.[25] Other economists, including J. S. Mill and J. M. Keynes, have questioned the wisdom of the presumption of insatiability and held out the view that the so-called economic problem might someday be solved, if only mankind is capable of recognizing its solution when and if the time comes. In his otherwise influential classic, Mill, speaking of the stationary state, obviously looked forward to a time when further quantitative economic progress would not be desired much less needed.

> I cannot, therefore, regard the stationary state of capital and wealth with the unaffected aversion so generally manifested towards it by political economists of the old school. I am inclined to believe that it would be, on the whole, a very considerable improvement on our present condition. I confess I am not

> charmed with the ideal of life held out by those who think that the normal state of human beings is that of struggling to get on; that the trampling, crushing, elbowing, and treading on each other's heels, which form the existing type of social life, are the most desirable lot of human kind, or anything but the disagreeable symptoms of one of the phases of industrial progress. ... I know not why it should be matter of congratulation that persons who are already richer than anyone needs to be, should have doubled their means of consuming things which give little or no pleasure except as representative of wealth. ...[26]

Keynes observed that 'in the long run ... *mankind is solving its economic problem*' and goes on to consider the question of insatiability in terms reminiscent of Veblen's invidious comparison or Marx's commodity fetishism.

> Now it is true that the needs of human beings may seem to be insatiable. But they fall into two classes – those needs which are absolute ..., and those which are relative in the sense that we feel them only if their satisfaction lifts us above, makes us feel superior to our fellows. Needs of the second class, those which satisfy the desire for superiority, may indeed be insatiable ...[27]

The needs for social esteem and even invidious distinction may be insatiable but it is not inevitable that they be expressed through an endless treadmill of commodity consumption. Moreover, insatiability based on invidy is a neurosis, a sickness, more to be pitied and cured than celebrated and legitimated as a primary social force. This is clearly the critique that Marxists and Veblenians make concerning a mature capitalist economy which is unable to put its vast productive power to use satisfying reasonable human needs and raising the degree of human freedom to epoch-making new levels. More recently, William Leiss has provided a remarkably incisive discussion on the relation of human needs to commodities that, in my estimation, fully bears out the Marxist and Veblenian traditions.[28]

TOWARD A NEW DEPARTURE

Polanyi's methodological concern is now clearly in hand. Recognition of the primacy of society in human life, that economic activity is social activity, necessitates a new departure in economic thought.

> Approaching the economic process from the vantage point of the new knowledge we have gained of the reality of society, we must say that there is no necessary relationship between economizing action and the empirical economy. The institutional structure of the economy need not compel, as with the market system, economizing actions. The implications of such an insight for all the social sciences which must deal with the economy could hardly be more far-reaching. Nothing less than a fundamentally different starting point for the analysis of the human economy as a social process is required. (*PAME*, pp. 117–18)

The basis of this departure is also clearly in view.

> It is our proposition that only the substantive meaning of economic is capable of yielding the concepts that are required by the social sciences for an investigation of all the empirical economies past and present. (*PAME*, p. 140)

If the approach to economic anthropology, economic history, and comparative economic systems is not to be fatally prefigured, that is, if the essential institutional analysis is to be made possible, the operative *gestalt* must be freed of the formalist prejudice. Lowe has offered a very apt and succinct way of posing the essential question of institutional analysis: 'What must we know in order to gain systematic understanding of the economic activities of a human group, and by what intellectual techniques can such "economic knowledge" be obtained?'[29]

As I have already suggested, the paralytic impact of the economistic fallacy is not limited to the methodology of economic anthropology, economic history, and comparative economic systems in a purely academic sense. For one thing, the fallacy robs society of a large part of the advantages to be gained through the comparison of economic systems, specifically, to know oneselves and one's situations better by coming to understand the character and situations of people in different circumstances. Consider the views of Morris Bornstein and Benjamin Ward on the value of comparative economic studies:

> [C]omparative economic studies can make a unique contribution to economics as a whole, by providing the perspective to overcome the parochialism inherent in economic thinking – on both theoretical and policy questions – based on the experience of a single economic system. The comparison of systems enriches the analyst's understanding of his own system, sharpening his appreciation of its merits and demerits and suggesting organizational and operational changes to improve its performance.[30]

> Piecemeal social engineering is not the only feasible engine of change. Thoroughgoing economic reorganization is the most spectacular instrument of economic control; it is widely advocated and rather widely practiced. Therefore even a little information, if it can be used to prevent a few of the grossest errors, may be of very great value.[31]

The comparison of economic systems can contribute to both theoretical and policy problems because it enables economists to widen their field of vision beyond their own limited institutional experience. Clearly, the ethnocentrism of the economistic fallacy must surely limit the ability of economists to realize this benefit of comparative economic study. Polanyi had this in mind, no doubt, and for him it was a matter of considerable urgency.

> The scholar's endeavor must be, first, to give clarity and precision to our concepts, so that we be enabled to formulate the problems of livelihood in terms fitted as closely as possible to the actual features of the situation in which we operate; and second to widen the range of principles and policies at our disposal through a study of the shifting place of the economy in human society and the methods by which civilizations of the past successfully engineered their great transitions.
>
> Accordingly, the theoretical task is to establish the study of man's livelihood on broad institutional and historical foundations. (*LM*, p. lvi)

This issues into a second area in which the impact of the economistic fallacy is of greater importance than the methodology of economic anthropology, history, and systems. The 'broad institutional and historical foundations' are, in Polanyi's view, to serve as the basis of a truly universal economic theory. A universal economic theory must have an empirical basis which is as close to universal as possible. To prefigure comparative institutional analysis in the manner of the economistic fallacy is to render impossible the development of this broad empirical basis. In this regard, it is worth noting that the narrow empirical basis of economic science is a recurrent theme of recent discussion of the current crisis of economics.[32] What is being suggested here is that amelioration of this empirical lacuna should not be limited to a given economic system, or even modern economic systems, but should instead aim at as wide a field of vision and experience as possible.

The substantive connotation of economic is universal because all human groups must somehow secure their livelihood by turning nature's laws to their advantage. Provisioning is universal but the added stricture that provisioning be efficient or maximizing is a question of empirical fact. Economy, in the formalist sense of calculativeness in the face of scarcity, may or may not be present. For the substantivist, like the economic sociologist, economic rationality must be considered as an institutionalized value.[33] Moreover, even if it is present, and widely so, in a given society, economic rationality does not exist in a vacuum but is fitted into a complex of values which cannot be assumed to be consistent or non-competitive with one another. A society may place great store in efficiency and be solidly committed to the economizing organization of its economic aspect, yet still find this value to be subordinate to other, conflicting values. Society may not like the character of its people if they are calculative and acquisitive, even though these traits serve the value of efficiency. This was, after all, a large part of the focus of the Romantic reaction to the dismal science of classical political economy.[34] Wordsworth scored a direct hit in this regard in his sonnet, 'Inside of King's College Chapel, Cambridge': 'high Heaven rejects the lore of nicely calculated less or more.' In Kenneth Boulding's terms, society may well value the heroic ethic more than the economic ethic.[35] At any rate, it is such questions which necessitate a societal perspective in economics. Only a focus on economy and society can reveal the critically important questions about the economy and human character.

Polanyi's conviction of the necessity of a universal economic theory founded upon a universal economic history is thoroughly practical in its inspiration. He was convinced that the great problems of modern times will yield to nothing less than such a universal perspective; or, better, that if democratic industrial society is to have any chance against the magnitude and multitude of its social problems, it must approach them with as wide a range of instruments as possible. It would be foolhardy and probably tragic if contemporary society were to neglect any possible tool of thought and action that might serve humankind in its hour of crisis. In terms sharply reminiscent of Veblen's desperately precarious institutional situation,[36] Polanyi warns of perilous adjustment and the pitfalls of avoidable difficulties, the dangers of which are greatly exacerbated by an obsolete wisdom and a paralytic mentality.

> This work is an economic historian's contribution to world affairs in a period of perilous transformation. Its aim is simple: to enlarge our freedom of creative adjustment, and thereby improve our chances of survival, the problem of man's material livelihood should be subjected to total reconsideration. (*LM*, p. xliii)

This total reconsideration, from a substantivist paradigm, must overturn the 'obsolete notions' and 'grievously incomplete understanding of the nature of the human economy' which are inherent in the economistic fallacy. The fallacy leaves the way clear for a 'marketing mind' or 'obsolete market mentality'. This mind set impacts a very broad, indeed total, range of theoretical and practical problems. Economistic thinking permeates public thinking and all the disciplines intent upon the study of man in the 'ordinary business of life' (see *LM*, pp. 5, 24, and 31; and, *PAME*, pp. 118–19). It was Polanyi's intent, through the contrast of the formal and substantive meanings of economic, and through the universal economic theory to be built on the substantivist reconstruction of the facts of economic life, to sweep away economism and clear the way for social economics.

> One simple recognition, from which all attempts at clarification of the place of the economy in society must start, is the fact that the term *economic*, as commonly used to describe a type of human activity, is a compound of two meanings. (*LM*, p. 19)
>
> The economistic fallacy, as we have called it, consists in a tendency to equate the human economy with its market form. Accordingly, to eliminate this bias, a radical clarification of the meaning of the word *economic* is required. (*LM*, p. 20)
>
> The use of the term "economic" is bedeviled by ambiguities.

> Economic theory has invested it with a time-bound connotation that renders it ineffective outside of the narrow confines of our market-dominated societies. Terms like supply, demand, and price should be replaced with wider terms such as resources, requirements, and equivalencies. The historian will then be able to compare the economic institutions of different periods and regions without running the danger of foisting upon the bare facts the market shape of things.
>
> Once out of the rubber cell of self-defeating notions, we can come to grips with realities. (*LM*, p. xl)

Polanyi's methodological critique of formalism was very practical in its motivation. His fundamental aim followed directly from his conviction that only through a reconsideration of the past could a new understanding of the present emerge by which the creation of a desirable future could be guided. The receding market pattern that he described in *The Great Transformation* left a vacuum that is as much social and cultural as economic. The rise of the market economy had necessarily implied the renovation of the social totality; the transcendence of that economy will also require the total reconstruction of everyday life and thought. Such a reconstruction will need to be guided by thinking that is not tainted by the market mentality.

> A critical survey of the catallactic definitions of trade, money and market should make available a number of concepts which form the raw material of the social sciences in their economic aspect. The bearing of this recognition on questions of theory, policy and outlook should be viewed in the light of the gradual institutional transformation that has been in progress since the first World War. Even in regard to the market system itself, the market as the sole frame of reference is somewhat out of date. Yet, as should be more clearly realized than it sometimes has been in the past, the market cannot be superseded as a general frame of reference unless the social sciences succeed in developing a wider frame of reference to which the market itself is referable. This indeed is our main intellectual task today in the field of economic studies. As we have attempted to show, such a conceptual structure will have to be grounded on the substantive meaning of economic. (*TMEE*, pp. 269–70)

In the next two chapters, I review Polanyi's effort to establish a wider frame of reference and his explanation of the receding market pattern that makes this 'our main intellectual task'.

3 Social and Economic Integration

As indicated in the previous chapter, Polanyi's historical and anthropological bent had a definite, eminently practical purpose. His intent was 'to make universal economic history the starting point of a comprehensive reconsideration of the problem of human livelihood' (*LM*, p. xxxix). This is the task for further research which Polanyi set in *The Great Transformation*. Its completion requires that 'general economic history be re-established on broad conceptual foundations' (*LM*, p. xxxix). In this chapter, I consider, first, the method for approaching this task, institutional analysis; and, second, the conceptual foundations that result, the forms of integration. Finally, I review Marshall Sahlins' application of this research programme to the ethnographic record of primitive economies.

INSTITUTIONAL ANALYSIS

In identifying the task of institutional analysis, Polanyi made clear the close relationship between the methodological animus of his work and the ideological problem of contemporary political economy:

> To shift in natural science from one conceptual framework to another is one thing; to do so in the social sciences is quite another. It is like rebuilding a house, foundation, walls, fittings and all, while continuing to live in it. We must rid ourselves of the ingrained notion that the economy is a field of experience of which human beings have necessarily always been conscious. To employ a metaphor, the facts of the economy were originally embedded in situations that were not in themselves of an economic nature. . . . The crystallization of the concept of the economy was a matter of time and history. But neither time nor history have

> provided us with those conceptual tools required to penetrate the maze of social relationships in which the economy was embedded. This is the task of what we will here call institutional analysis. (*TMEE*, p. 242)

Again, the critical import which attaches to general economic history and its method of institutional analysis is the need to throw off the obsolete market mentality.

It is also clear that the essential task of institutional analysis is conceptual or theoretical, notwithstanding its methodological commitment to comparative, descriptive studies of concrete social arrangements. It is important to note that the successful completion of this essentially theoretical task by this method requires not only much on the part of the investigators but something of the data as well. As Harry Pearson noted, 'the ability to generalize and predict depends, with this method, upon the emergence of common patterns in the institutionalized operations' (*TMEE*, p. 309). It was, in fact, one of the major findings reported in *Trade and Market in the Early Empires* that the ethnographic record shows only a few patterns by which the economy has been organized in human society.

> Thus the main task of this book is conceptual: it argues that only a small number of alternative patterns for organizing man's livelihood exist and it provides us with tools for the examination of nonmarket economies. . . .
>
> Technological progress is cumulative and unbounded, but economic organization is not. There are only a few general ways in which the economy may be organized. It is this limitation of the possible patterns of economic organization and their effective combinations which gives to the thoughts and data offered here some topicality. In the receding rule of the market in the modern world, shapes reminiscent of the economic organization of earlier times make their appearance. Of course we stand firmly committed to the progress and freedoms which are the promise of modern society. But a purposeful use of the past may help us to meet our present overconcern with economic matters and to achieve a level of human integration, that comprises the economy, without being absorbed in it.
>
> It is this which makes economic history come alive and throw light on the changing roles of economies in history and society. (*TMEE*, pp. xvii–xviii)

Institutional patterns are recurrent because the human element is recurrent. If the ethnographic record displayed no boundedness nor recurrence of organizational patterns, it would retain some interest per se but its relevance to the central institutional problem of the present, the receding market, would be virtually nil. Without recurrence of patterns in the past, there would be no reason to suppose that it would be of use in anticipating and shaping the future. With recurrence, it is reasonable to assume that the patterns of the past contain the key to the patterns of the future.

Taken together the receding market and the small number of patterns give Polanyi's research programme a rather definite shape. By conceptualizing these patterns and reporting on their operating in many different historical settings, Polanyi and his colleagues sought to pave the way for a more general theory of economy and society than is possible under the sway of the market mentality. In its preoccupation with the mechanics of individual choice and exchange, the market theory abstracts from the underlying sociological framework and fails to delve into concrete questions of personality formation, power, and the like.[1] Since this underlying complex varies across space and especially time, the market theory is of limited value in comparative analysis. As Daniel Fusfeld remarked, 'the social scientist who deals with cross-cultural problems is inevitably concerned with institutions and cannot use effectively a set of tools which deliberately abstracts from the institutional framework' (*TMEE*, p. 344). And, given the receding market pattern and the rise of the so-called mixed economy, all research in a sense bears the onus of being concerned with cross-cultural problems. The limitations of the market theory thus become intensely practical as does the need for a social economic theory expressing 'the reality of society that is replacing in our day the fading image of an individualistic atomism' (*TMEE*, p. 374).

The link between the reality or primacy of society and its reproduction on the one hand, and the economic organization and its place in society on the other, is emphasized by the substantive conception of the economy as an *instituted process* which functions to secure social reproduction. This substantive concept of the economy is the starting point of institutional analysis. In this view, the economy 'can be briefly (if not engagingly) defined as an instituted process of interaction between man and his environment, which results in a continuous supply of want-satisfying material means' (*PAME*, p. 145). By process, with its emphasis on change and movement, Polanyi referred to the technological mediation of humanity with the rest of nature. This is humanity's essential materiality. Institutedness refers to the other major dimension of human life, its essential sociality. The substantive or materialist conception rivets attention to the institutional and technological interface between human society and non-human nature. It also focuses attention on the place of the economy in society. 'The study of the shifting place occupied by the economy in society is therefore no other than the study of the manner in which the economic process is instituted at different times and places. This requires a special tool box' (*PAME*, p. 148). Polanyi developed this tool box by starting 'from the way in which the economy acquires unity and stability, that is the interdependence and recurrence of its parts. This is achieved through a very few patterns, which may be called forms of integration' (*PAME*, pp. 148–9).

Institutional analysis is then concerned with the integration of economic activities with one another and with other social activities, and with classifying economies in accordance with the manner in which integration is sustained.

> Of the various ways in which economies can be classified empirically, that one should be given preference which avoids prejudging the significant issues arising from the problem of the place occupied by the economy in the society as a whole. The issues which stand out are those involving the relations of the economic process to the political and cultural spheres of the society at large. To avoid prejudging these issues, it is suggested here that economies be grouped according to the form of integration dominant in each of them. Integration is present in the economic process to the extent that those movements of goods and persons which overcome the effect of space, time, and occupational differentials are institutionalized so as to create interdependence among the movements. Thus, for example, regional differences within a territory, the time span between sowing and harvesting, or the specialization of labor is overcome by whatever movements of the respective crops, manufactures, and labor make their distribution more effective. Forms of integration thus designate the institutionalized movements through which the elements of the economic process – from material resources and labour to the transportation, storage, and distribution of goods – are connected. (*LM*, p. 35)

The dominance of a form of integration is to be found in the organization of land and labour.

> A tribal community is characterized by the integration of land and labor into the economy through ties of kinship. In feudal society, the ties of fealty determine the fate of land and of the labor that goes with it. In the floodwater empires, land was largely distributed (and sometimes redistributed) by temple or palace, as was labor, at least in its dependent form. The modern rise of the market to a ruling force in the economy can be traced by noting the extent to which land and food were mobilized through exchange and labor was turned into a commodity to be purchased in the market. (*LM*, p. 43)

This emphasis is also to be found in Marx who stressed the labour element but always with the labourer's relationship to his 'natural workshop' in mind. It is found also in the conservative view of economic history, as indicated in Benjamin Ward's rendition of 'the conservative economic world view' concerning the distinctive character of the nineteenth-century social economy.

> In the nineteenth century a new kind of society emerged and began a process of relatively peaceful conquest of the world. This was the thoroughgoing trading society, and England and the United States were its proving grounds. The particularly novel feature of this form of society lay in the marketization of land, labor, and capital. In earlier times each of these factors of production had been subject to occasional sale from time to time, but never before had an integrated market system involving all three of the basic factors developed.[2]

A given integrational form can operate only in the context of a fairly definite institutional structure. Market exchange as a means of integration requires a very different social, cultural, and political environment than reciprocity or redistribution. This is only to say that individuals must learn to behave economically, that they must be socialized or acculturated to perform in the economy. It is important to note that this is not a matter merely of attitudes or psychological inclinations.

The effective functioning of forms of integration depends upon

> the presence of definite institutional structures, and it has long been tempting for some to assume that such structures are the result of certain kinds of personal attitudes. Adam Smith's "propensity to truck, barter, and exchange" is perhaps the most famous example. It is not true, however, that individual acts and attitudes simply add up to create the institutional structures that support the forms of integration.
>
> The supporting structures, their basic organization, and their validation spring from the societal sphere. (*LM*, p. 37)

In others words, institutional analysis is more sociological than psychological: 'if historical perspective means anything at all, it is that individual motives and personalities are quite unimportant compared with institutional changes' (*LM*, p. 240). The comparative analysis of social change and evolution is focused upon social structure because this structure selects or represses particular attitudes or motivations: 'single out whatever motive [e.g., generosity or gain] you please and organize production in such a manner as to make that motive the individual's incentive *to produce*, you will have induced a picture of man as altogether absorbed by that motive' (*LM*, p. 11).

This is the root of Polanyi's insistence that so-called human nature changes but little in the process of social evolution. If men appear here to be generous, there selfish, it is not their basic natures that are different but their social organization.

> Take the case of tribal society. The individual's economic interest is rarely paramount, for the community keeps all its members from starving unless it is itself borne down by catastrophe. . . . The maintenance of social ties, on the other hand, is crucial. First, because by disregarding the accepted code of honor, or generosity, the individual cuts himself off from the community and becomes an outcast; second, because, in the long run, all social obligations are reciprocal, and their fulfillment serves also the individual's give-and-take interests best. Such a situation must exert a continuous pressure on the individual to eliminate economic self-interest from his consciousness. . . . This attitude is reinforced by the frequency of communal activities such as partaking of food from the common catch. . . . The premium set on generosity is so great . . . in terms of social prestige as to make any other behavior than that of utter self-forgetfulness simply not pay. Personal

> character has little to do with the matter. . . . The human passions, good or bad, are merely directed towards noneconomic ends. (*GT*, pp. 46–7)

The presence of this or that motive is, then, not the important factor in institutional analysis. Rather, it is the institutional structure in which motives operate. 'These observations help make clear how and why individual personal attitudes so often fail to have societal effects in the absence of given societal conditions' (*LM*, p. 38). For example, the motive of gain, the calculated pursuit of individual economic interest, may well be ubiquitous in human history but its historical maturity or predominant social position occurs only in market capitalism because it is there instituted as the principal incentive to economic activity. With this in mind, one can appreciate J. M. Clark's remark that 'the worst evil is to deny those incentives which represent what man recognizes as best in him. If selfish incentives cease to work, that is a failure: if unselfish incentives have no opportunity to work, that is a tragedy'.[3]

Like other institutionalists, especially Thorstein Veblen, Polanyi found the key to institutional analysis in the literature of anthropology. In *Trade and Market in the Early Empires*, Conrad Arensberg's article 'Anthropology as History' indicates why Polanyi stressed anthropology and general economic history. Both disciplines are empirical and 'both deal with events and occurrences, not with man's nature or the timeless necessities' (*TMEE*, p. 98). In other words, Harry Pearson's, in 'what might be called "institutional" analysis, the economy in its concrete manifestations is the subject of interest' (*TMEE*, p. 309). As Arensberg points out, anthropology with this concrete, empirical bent does not take as its point of departure the individual with any of his various complement of physiological or psychological attributes. Instead, the focus is on society as a system in which the basic units of analysis are 'patterns of interaction' (*TMEE*, p. 100). This is Polanyi's primacy of society and, as Arensberg notes,

> anthropology is deeply committed to this priority of social patterns in any scheme for the understanding of the substantive economies of the human record. Our discipline is preconditioned to derive specific motivations, whether "economic" or otherwise, from such arrangements rather than from abstract human nature and needs. But it also sees these patterns and arrangements as historically

> achieved rather than as consequences of the play of general forces of human nature or circumstance . . . . (*TMEE*, pp. 100–1)

This enables clarification of Polanyi's notes on human nature. There is no need to deny the presence of some abstract, timeless nature of man; it is necessary only to insist that this nature is relatively constant and that variations in the human condition must therefore be explained by social context. After dividing the relevant factors, into physiological, psychological, and social, Terence Hopkins notes:

> the non-social aspects of the economic process appear largely as constant processes which in no wise determine the variations in human activities although they just as certainly are present in all concrete actions . . . . (*TMEE*, p. 294)

> To explain these variations in men's economic activities, then, one must turn to the wider system of social actions, the society, of which the economy as a social process is a part. For these economic activities . . . are the product . . . of the ordered ways of group living, of the patterns of interaction; and the coherence that the activities clearly manifest results primarily from [their] being a part of this system of interaction patterns.
>
> The economic process is an 'instituted process', then, in the obvious sense that an essential part of it is also a part of a social system – that part composed of the activities of men contributing to the supply of material means. The patterning manifested by these 'economic activities' derives from the same source that the patterning of any set of social actions derives, namely, the process of institutionalization. (*TMEE*, p. 295)

This shows clearly why Polanyi stressed institutions over attitudes and why he adopted the substantive view of the economy as an instituted process for provisioning.

Arensberg's reference to historically achieved patterns and arrangements indicates much about the task of anthropology and institutional analysis. These patterns must not only be identified in terms of their historical–geographical presence but also accounted for in terms of their social function. This means that their connection to other elements of the social system must be explained, and the processes which assure their continuation identified. This concrete accounting is necessary because 'a culture pattern is a concrete thing, whose presence or absence is an historical fact and whose emergence is an historical event' (*TMEE*, p. 101). There is therefore no substitute for spelling out 'in faithful, empirical detail all observable and checkable dovetailing of transmitted action, interaction, meaning and context which makes up any culture pattern' (*TMEE*, p. 102). The focus must also be dynamic or evolutionary to capture the essential element of continuity. Institutional analysis therefore must be empirical, functional, holistic, and evolutionary.

Institutional analysis must also be comparative if a theoretical core is to emerge. Harry Pearson: 'The ability to generalize and predict depends, with this method, upon the emergence of common patterns in the institutionalized operations' (*TMEE*, p. 309). These common patterns can only be identified by comparative analysis. As Daniel Fusfeld observes, the methodological task of institutional analysis

> requires not only empirical studies of production and distribution that center on economic institutions and their relationship to the larger social structure, but also a willingness to theorize about the place of the economic system in society and not merely about individual choices. . . . The real task is nothing less than the building of a cross-cultural economics based on the substantive problems of production and distribution rather than on formal problems of choice. (*TMEE*, pp. 354–5).

The task is largely one of constructing a theory anew because the formalist orientation of extant economic theory severely limits its usefulness to institutional analysis, which must depart from a substantivist orientation if a genuine comparative economics is to be formulated. In this view, 'the "economy" is conceived as *a component of culture* rather than *a kind of human action*, the material life process of society rather than a need-satisfying process of individual behavior. Our purpose is not to analyze entrepreneurs but to compare cultures' (*SAE*, p. 186n).

The comparative method, founded on careful documentation of substantive historical situations, will enable the institutional analyst to treat economic institutions as culture traits, i.e. as expressions of values or meaning stemming from definite patterns of social interaction. 'It is in this way alone, in treating them as cultural traits, that we can legitimately spell out the cultural dynamics and reconstruct the true history of economic institutions' (*TMEE*, p. 107). Arensberg goes on to refer to a 'rewon history', which phrasing is very suggestive of a fundamental theme of this work, to wit, much can be learned from the past, even and perhaps especially the remote past, about the place of economy in society if that past is not prefigured by ethnocentric presumption. The formalist perspective prefigures all economic systems as being first, foremost, and last concerned with *the* economic problem of efficient resource allocation and equitable distribution of the products that result. This is, of course, the hallmark of modern, especially market, economies. At worst, this ethnocentrism leads to the presumption that market exchanges must have existed in the past; at best, it leads to the search for functional equivalents of the market process. This notion of functional equivalents may be referred to as the *implicit-market model*. It is much more subtle and poses a more formidable challenge to substantivism than the naive presumption that explicit market systems must exist anywhere the economic problem is faced, to wit, everywhere. The implicit conception maintains that, since economic choices are made, some calculations *vis-à-vis* relative values must have been involved, even if there are no explicit market prices. The choices would probably have been based on relatively inferior information in the absence of explicit prices, but they would be no less economic in the formal sense simply by virtue of being thusly constrained by ignorance or uncertainty. The corollary argument is often made that the market is superior because it provides explicit and presumably more accurate information for the inveterate practice of individual calculation – the market is consonant with human nature.

For example, in a system of reciprocity an individual may be said to choose to share his produce based on a calculation of the relative values of sharing versus hoarding. If he shares, he makes or solidifies social relations which he can rationally expect to yield future benefits in the form of reciprocal sharing. If he hoards, he reserves his own produce for his own future use. If the social exclusion and its economic consequences owing to disclosure of furtive hoarding is extreme, then the relative valuation may be expected to indicate that sharing is the prudent course of action. The use of social and political sanctions therefore constrains the individual's economic choices in a way that proponents of the market and personal freedom connection abhor in principle. At any rate, speculation about the individual's psyche would not seem to be as important as studying the institutions which mold his behaviour toward sharing.

In contrast, substantive institutional analysis

> is not a study of the functional equivalents of our economic institutions in other cultures and societies. It is doubtful indeed whether beyond subsistence man has had any universal economic problems; rather his problems arise, like his values, from his institutions and their evolutions. To restrict a study of economic institutions to the functional equivalents among societies, and to neglect the discovery that they are also in part culture patterns and behave like these, would be to falsify the facts. (Arensberg, *TMEE*, p. 110)

This is not to deny that there is some, not to specify half, truth to the notion of functional equivalents. Economic institutions at all times and places do assign productive resources to their tasks and do mete out the products among people in the society. But the notion of functional equivalents says far more than this. With its idiom of choice, allocation, and distribution, it suggests the presence of calculation, maximization, even greed, and herein lies the economistic fallacy's eclipse of institutional analysis.

> Certainly . . . we can find that gift-giving does the same things for human individual and social life as does the market. Both are mechanisms for distribution and survival. But they are different mechanisms, based on very different social arrangements, in many ways opposite cultural and institutional elaborations. Presumably as well they have very different antecedents, advantages, and limitations. (*TMEE*, p. 112)

These different mechanisms and arrangements may have very different implications for the quality and context of human life. It is the essence of Polanyi's research programme, and, I think, the institutional dilemma of democratic industrial society, to find ways and means of getting a livelihood which are less disruptive of lives and less detrimental to the quality of life. It is this which vests the task of learning from the past with its practical import, indeed, urgency. Institutional invention and innovation, like its technical counterpart, is a process of new departures embarked upon by newly combining elements of the old (*TMEE*, p. 111). Ethnocentrism severely limits the elemental pool from which such recombinations may occur because it sees *x* everywhere and takes no notice of *y* and *z*. It therefore restricts society's capacity of institutional imagination, vision, and innovation.

For substantive institutional analysis, to be as clear as possible, *the* economic problem is less one of efficiency or optimization than of sufficiency. The economy is viewed as the aspect of human activity which functions to materially reproduce society as a going concern or integrated culture. This is, I think, the basis of Clarence Ayres' refusal to charge Institutional economics with providing alternative answers to the mainstream questions about relative prices and their allocative function. The task of Institutionalism lies elsewhere; it is to promulgate an utterly different and probably contradictory perspective on the character of the economic process.[4]

FORMS OF INTEGRATION

As already indicated, Polanyi concluded that there were only a small number of institutional patterns by which human societies have organized their economies. More specifically, he identified three forms of integration: reciprocity, redistribution, and exchange, to which he added the principle of householding.

Consider first *market exchange* as a form of integration. Due to its familiarity and the extensive discussion given this form of integration in the next chapter I can be relatively brief at this point. A key point in Polanyi's view is that exchange, in order to function as an integrative mechanism, 'requires the support of a system of price-making markets' (*PAME*, p. 154). The mere existence of exchange and prices is not sufficient because exchange which takes place at administered or treaty-given prices is integrated not by the market but by the politics of administration and treaty. In other words, exchange as an integrative mechanism implies a self-regulating system of markets and an economy predominantly directed by market prices. This requires price-making markets which in turn presupposes a bargaining process which serves to determine prices.

> Exchange is a two-way movement of goods between persons oriented toward the gain ensuing for each from the resulting terms. In simpler terms, barter is the behavior of persons who exchange goods on the assumption that each makes the most of it.

> Higgling and haggling are of the essence here, since there is no other way each person can make sure he is gaining as much as possible from the bargain. Haggling, in this case is not the result of some human frailty, but a behavior pattern logically required by the mechanism of the market. (*LM*, p. 42)

The market participant must be intent upon bargaining so as to generate a price that is as favourable to his interest as possible. This is Adam Smith's higgling and haggling which is indeed pivotal to the operation of a market economy. It should also be noted that barter as a behavioural pattern must be widespread for price-making markets to exist. 'It is usually not realized that random acts of barter would not, by themselves, produce prices unless a market pattern were in existence that made the bartering intent of the persons effective' (*LM*, p. 42). This reiterates a point stressed above. Psychological motives operate in an institutional milieu. 'The market pattern is never traceable to the mere desire of individuals to "truck, barter, and exchange"' (*LM*, p. 42).

The market economy institutionalizes the barter mentality by its emphasis on scarcity. The formalist view expresses the economic thought and ideology, indeed, the culture of the market economy. Culture in this sense means shared meaning, guiding principles, or the symbols which explain social reality to individuals and provide them with an intelligible model to guide their behaviour. In a market economy, the cultural reality is scarcity and the moral obligation to calculate and make the best of limited resources. 'Insufficiency of material means becomes the explicit, calculable starting point of all economic activity' (*SAE*, p. 4). In this mentality, for the individual 'every acquisition is simultaneously a deprivation' (*SAE*, p. 4). The resulting behaviour pattern is familiar to us – the motive of gain, the minimizing of expenditure of money or effort for a given outcome, or the maximizing of outcome for a given expenditure.

However, for a wide range of economies prior to the modern period, ethnographers agree on the following:

> The absence of the motive of gain, the absence of the principle of laboring for remuneration; the absence of the principle of least effort; and, especially, the absence of any separate and distinct institution based on economic motives. But how, then, is order in production and distribution ensured? The answer is provided in

> the main by two principles of behavior not primarily associated with economics: reciprocity and redistribution. (*GT*, p. 47)

Dalton defines *reciprocity* as the 'obligatory gift- and counter gift-giving between persons who stand in some socially defined relationship to one another' (*TPE*, p. 71). Reciprocity may be informally instituted in the manner of persistent and ritualized exchanging of gifts. It may be more formally instituted in highly ritual relationships. It requires a great deal of symmetrical division of the group into various subgroups. Thusly divided into groups, 'reciprocity means that members of one group act toward members of another group as members of that group or a third or fourth group act toward them' (*TMEE*, p. 222).

Reciprocity is extremely difficult to grasp for the modern mind. This is especially true given ethnocentrism. Examples of reciprocity may look like primitive exchange. Division of labour being limited by the extent of the market after the fashion of Adam Smith, these examples may appear to be merely lowly developed barter or exchange. Reciprocal gift-giving is easily misinterpreted in this way as quid pro quo in *statu nascendi*. 'In primitive communities reciprocity occurs as a vital feature of the economy. . . . But reciprocity in householding, however general, remains invisible to the modern observer who would notice economic phenomena only if they were reducible to exchange' (*DST*, p. xx). Although vital to the economy, reciprocity is not solely or principally economic, certainly not in the formalist sense nor even in the substantive sense. The social or political function of reciprocity always exists and may be dominant. In an extreme examples, as Polanyi observed, 'occasionally the identically same object is exchanged back and forth between the partners, thus depriving the transaction of any conceivable economic purpose or meaning. . . . The sole purpose of the exchange is to draw relationships closer by strengthening the ties of reciprocity' (*PAME*, p. 90). The binding function of reciprocity in this extreme example is evident. The purpose of exchanging the same object back and forth in some ceremonial fashion would be to underscore and reinforce the belongingness of the two parties to the group. Polanyi, noting that nothing 'could show better the meaning of reciprocity', quotes Aristotle from the *Nichomachian Ethics*:

> "The very existence of the state depends on such acts of proportionate reciprocity . . . failing which no sharing happens

> and it is the sharing which binds us together. This is why we set up a shrine of the graces in a public place to remind men to return a kindness; for that is a special characteristic of Greece, since it is a duty not only to repay a service done, but another time to take the initiative in doing a service oneself." (*PAME*, p. 110)

Aristotle also referred to a goodwill which must exist in any kind of community. This goodwill or *philia* expresses itself in reciprocity (*PAME*, p. 152).

Nonetheless, it is important to stress that reciprocity has a distinctly economic function. Binding is directly functional in an economic sense because social bonds are inherently integrating. They bring people closer together, render their activities intelligible to one another, and thus integrate their behaviour, economic and otherwise. Moreover, sharing carries out an important distributive function to secure livelihood for those in a human group who have failed to produce their own. The Old Testament, in many ways a series of tribal documents, is replete with remonstrances to share with the poor and to treat others in the group as one would have them treat oneself. The economic function of sharing was even more explicitly recognized in the medieval world view with its Catholic ideological or cultural basis. Charity was an explicit social obligation and was especially important to the personal salvation of the wealthy. This thinking evolved from Jesus' dictum that for the wealthy man to achieve salvation he would have to give away all his possessions and a similar sentiment that it would be easier for a camel to get through the eye of a needle than for a rich man to get into heaven. For practical purposes, for the ordinary run of people, those that did not aspire to be priests and achieve perfection on earth, the obligation became one of sharing wealth with the less fortunate rather than giving away all wealth. In addition, much of the discussion in medieval doctrine on the just price, usury, and the legitimation of the businessman also involves reciprocity. To lend at interest to a needy man is to violate reciprocity and to be uncharitable. Afterall, the lender may some day be in a similarly desperate strait and need assistance. To gain unduly from an exchange is to fail to reciprocate value for value. The gain of a businessman could be legitimated if used for charity or public purposes.

The last mentioned brings to mind Aristotle's insistence upon *liberality*. Aristotle defended private property on the basis of its necessity to developing personal character. In addition to the independence and responsibility associated with private property, Aristotle insisted that a man must have property if he is to practise liberality in its disposition. In this view wealth is pursued in order to be shared in parties, feasts, or public construction. Citizens are expected to reciprocate; hence, reciprocity may be an incentive to produce as in many primitive societies where wealth is sought to be shared or displayed in some public purpose.

Perhaps the best way for the modern mind to understand reciprocity is to consider social situations in which reciprocity continues to be very important. Modern man, after all, exchanges gifts on occasions such as Christmas, birthdays, graduations, weddings, and the like. This gift-giving is regulated to a large extent by the social relationships involved and not on the basis of any quid pro quo in terms of equivalency. There is an expectation of reciprocation but it is not a definite, equivalent reciprocation but one which is indefinite and regulated almost entirely by the occasion and the social positions of the people involved.

To take another example, consider the situation when a new family moves into a neighbourhood. The existing residents may well welcome the new neighbours with a meal or some other evidence of hospitality. The new neighbours would be expected to reciprocate in a reasonable period of time but certainly not with any certifiably equivalent gesture. In other words, it would be gauche to invite the existing residents to dinner on the very next night and even more so to serve a meal of identical value in an economic sense. Much the same kind of situation exists in entertaining friends or inviting friends to this or that social function. Reciprocation is expected but it is indefinite, nonequivalent, and regulated by the nature of the social relationships.

The key point is that the social relationships involved are paramount and definitive. These are face-to-face, familistic, personal relations – the closest thing in our current social science terminology is community. In these personal relations, reputation, congeniality, and the like are pivotal. The importance and rather difficult thing to envision is that in primitive society the economy was integrated within this community process. As Polanyi points out (*GT*, pp. 47–8) there exists in such settings an extreme publicity so that the participants in the group know of each other's achievements and shortcomings. The obligation to share is enforced by this publicity and the social, i.e. personal sanctions exercised against someone who refuses to share. Moreover, the incentive to produce is as likely as not one of reputation. The individual is rewarded for his efforts or penalized for his shortcomings by the extent of his reputation rather than by any direct material reward or deprivation.

Redistribution as an integrative mechanism involves obligatory transfers to some central authority. 'Redistribution entails obligatory payments of material items, money objects or labor services to some socially recognized center, usually king, chief, or priest, who reallocates portions of what he receives to provide community services (such as defense or feast), and to reward specific persons' (*TPE*, p. 73). 'Redistribution means that the produce of the group is brought together, either physically or by appropriation, and then parcelled out again among the members' (*TMEE*, p. 223). Clearly centricity is a necessary institutional pattern for the operation of redistribution. The central authority can be political or religious in its basis. The authority utilizes the transfers to meet its own requirements, those of public life and structures in general, and as a store against emergency situations, whether famine or war. Redistribution functions to integrate the economic activities where division of labour exists or when harvest and consumption are separate intertemporally. In hunting or fishing societies, it functions to smooth out the variability of success.

Redistribution is probably easier to comprehend to the modern mind given its relation to the nation-state and the obvious overcoming of division of labour by administrative procedure. Nonetheless, it is important to keep the personal or social milieu in mind when considering redistribution as it operates in premodern societies.

> Economically, it is an essential part of the existing system of division of labor, of foreign trading, of taxation for public purposes, of defense provisions. But these functions of an economic system proper are completely absorbed by the intensely vivid experiences which offer superabundant, noneconomic motivation for every act performed in the frame of the social system as a whole. (*GT*, p. 48)

The social function of redistribution is intermingled with its economic function and may dominate the latter. Redistribution serves to emphasize the unity of the group and the authority of its central figure. The individual's belonging to the group is therefore reinforced. As far as the authority of a central figure, I am reminded of Veblen's frequent discussion of the ceremonial visibility of a tribal chieftain, religious entity, or some other institutional idol. The tribute paid to such a central figure functions to evidence and reaffirm the figure's exalted status. Even the subsequent redistribution of tributes to members of the group may not be solely a matter of economic function since it serves as well to evidence the idol's beneficence and reinforce the loyalty of the members of the group to the idol and to one another.

The key failure of the modern welfare state may indeed be the neglect of this vivid personal relationship to the state. The result is a decline of *civitas* and a tendency to view the state as a tool for the pursuit of one's private interest.[5] The possibility of a disembedded polity – a polity above and separate from the personal and meaningful context of everyday life – is a serious question which Polanyi apparently neglected, despite its being in a very real sense the expected outcome of Polanyi's own theoretical work. If the market economy destroys social bonds and creates individuals excessively bent upon their own private gain, then it follows that these social characters would utilize the political process for their private ends. However, given Polanyi's discussion of the stalemate in democratic industrial society and the subsequent rise of fascism, on which I elaborate in Chapter 5, it seems certain that Polanyi was aware of the problem to some degree.

The principle of *householding* refers to production carried out for direct household use. Useful examples of householding are the independent peasant farmer in Europe or the yeoman farmer on the American frontier. The specific institutional form to which the concept is applicable need not be the household of the nuclear family. The Greek city state and medieval manor displayed strong elements of householding. The key point is not the size or social location of the unit in question, but is instead its orientation to economic activity.

> Its pattern is the closed group. Whether the very different entities of the family or the settlement or the manor form the self-sufficient unit, the principle is invariably the same, namely, that of producing and storing for the satisfaction of the wants of the members of the group. The principle is as broad in its application as either reciprocity or redistribution. The nature of the institutional nucleus is indifferent: it may be sex as with the patriarchal family, locality as with the village settlement, or

political power as with the seigneurial manor. Nor does the internal organization of the group matter. It may be as despotic as the Roman *familia* or as democratic as the South Slav zadruga; as large as the great domains of the Carolingian magnates or as small as the average peasant holding of Western Europe. (*GT*, p. 53)

Householding is characterized by self-sufficiency in the substantive sense. Economic activity is motivated by the necessity of provisioning and production is carried out with an eye to its direct use by members of the group. So also is distribution tied to the substantive economy.

Louis Henry Morgan called the program of the domestic economy "communism in living." The name seems apposite, for householding is the highest form of economic sociability: "from each according to his abilities and to each according to his needs" – from the adults that which they are charged by the division of labor; to them, but also to the elders, the children, the incapacitated, regardless of their contributions, that which they require. The sociological precipitate is a group with an interest and destiny apart from those outside and a prior claim on the sentiments and resources of those within. (*SAE*, p. 94)

One note is of possible interest. Polanyi argued that householding usually involves the supporting institutional pattern of autarchy (*GT*, p. 55). No doubt he was using autarchy in the sense of self-sufficiency which is usually spelled autarky, since he mentions the democratic internal organization in one instance. He was elsewhere more explicit when he said that 'autarchy may be said to be the capacity to subsist without dependence on resources from outside' (*PAME*, p. 96). However, it seems that autarchy in the normal sense of the personal and virtually absolute power of some central figure is also historically associated with the household; for example, the paternalism of the father in the nuclear family or the aristocratic lord of the medieval manor.

It is not at all clear in Polanyi's discussions whether householding is meant to be a fourth principle or pattern of integration. In *The Great Transformation* (ch. 4), he appears to give it equal footing with the other three integrative mechanisms. However, elsewhere he refers to householding as a possible fourth pattern of integration, but then states that 'formally this is actually redistribution on a smaller scale' (*PAME*, pp. 307–8). In my own view householding is not an integrative mechanism in the same sense as the other three because it provides no added form of integration. Householding must itself be integrated by one of the three mechanisms. Even within the nuclear household where intimacy makes integration appear automatic, reciprocity and redistribution no doubt operate. In larger scale householding, where intimacy is less, the use of these integrative mechanisms within the household unit becomes more evident. Moreover, in these larger scale situations, there is usually small scale households within the larger unit. Here the problem of integrating interhousehold behaviour clearly would require the other mechanisms. Finally, it would seem that householding is an essential feature of most economies integrated by the other three mechanisms. This may be what Dalton had in mind when he insists that Polanyi regarded reciprocity, redistribution, and exchange as 'modes of transaction, not as designations for entire economies or economic systems' (*PAME*, p. 153n).

In general, as one would expect from the above discussion of psychology and institutions, the required behaviour patterns associated with each of the integrative mechanisms can be achieved by a wide range of cultural realities. The meaning that the individual attaches to his behaviour and its place relative to the behaviour of others is very relativistic and displays immense variations. I believe this is so even of individuals pursuing self-gain in a market economy, but it is certainly true of the other institutional patterns. Speaking of these earlier patterns, Polanyi observed that 'the orderly production and distribution of goods was secured through a great variety of individual motives disciplined by general principles of behavior. . . . Custom and law, magic and religion cooperated in inducing the individual to comply with rules of behavior which, eventually, ensured his functioning in the economic system' (*GT*, p. 55).

The discussion of nonmarket patterns of integration brings up what is perhaps Polanyi's most insistent point: the embeddedness of economic activity in the general social fabric so that there is no separate economic sphere with a distinct set of motives and functions. The ethnographic record points instead to economic activity being motivated by the individual's general social location and interests.

> The outstanding discovery of recent historical and anthropological research is that man's economy, as a rule, is submerged in his social relationships. He does not act so as to

> safeguard his individual interest in the possession of material goods; he acts so as to safeguard his social standing, his social claims, his social assets. He favors material goods only insofar as they serve this end. Neither the process of production nor that of distribution is linked to specific economic interests attached to possession of goods; but every single step in that process is geared to a number of social interests which eventually ensure that the required step be taken. (*GT*, p. 46)

The social relations involved are usually face-to-face, familistic, and informal. As noted above, in current usage the word *community* comes closest to the mark. It is important to stress that the term is employed here to mean a wide and persistent range of relations and interests, in contrast to the relatively narrow connotation of such phrases as community of interest. The latter are best described as associations because they are oriented around specific interests or objectives. MacIver, building upon Tönnies' famous distinction, has made the point well:

> Association is a group specifically organized for the purpose of an interest or group of interests which its members have in common. . . . Community is a circle of people who live together, who belong together, so that they share not this or that particular interest, but a whole set of interests wide enough and comprehensive enough to include their lives. (Quoted in *TPE*, p. 63)

In such societies, it is social relations and considerations which determine economic activities and relations. This has been well described by Raymond Firth with respect to primitive societies:

> In primitive communities, the individual as an economic factor is personalized, not anonymous. He tends to hold his economic position in virtue of his social position.
>
> The ties between producers tend to reach out beyond this common interest in the act of production and its rewards alone. A production relationship is often only one facet of a social relationship. . . . Economic relations can be understood only as a part of a scheme of social relations. . . . Economic anthropology deals primarily with the economic aspects of the social relations of persons.

> From each according to his status obligations in the social system, to each according to his rights in that system. (Quoted in *TPE*, pp. 62, 65, and 71)

In the economies Firth was describing, the key questions of allocation and distribution, namely, what to produce, how to produce it, and for whom to produce it, are answered not by any specifically economic process but by the social process in general. This is the significance of Firth's reference to economic anthropology as the study of the economic aspects of social behaviour rather than as the study of economic behaviour.

In such economies, traditional social economies, the concept of choice has an entirely different meaning from that which obtains in the market capitalist society. Dalton has expressed the point well:

> Those who perceive an economy as a cluster of individual behavers frequently equate whatever economic activities the behavers undertake with explicit *choice* of those activities, and believe that such choice affirms the economics textbook dictum that in all economies there must be choice of what to produce, how to produce it, and who is to get how much of what is produced. This way of introducing the topics of resource allocation, production functions, and income distribution in industrial capitalism to beginning students in economics is useful because the individual households and firms in national market economies such as our own are confronted with many explicit choices. . . . These alternative choices are subject to fine calculation because industrial capitalism makes extensive use of money and pricing, and because there are real alternatives among which economic choices can be made without calling down social opprobium. . . .
>
> In subsistence (non-market) economies, the question of choice among real alternatives does not arise in such explicit fashion. A Trobriand Islander learns and follows the rules of *economy* in his society almost like an American learns and follows the rules of *language* in his. An American is born into an English-speaking culture. In no sense does he "choose" to speak English because no real alternative is presented to him. So too, the Trobriander is born into a yam-growing economy. He does not "choose" to plant yams rather than broccoli. (*EDSC*, p. 188)

The choices made in such economies are both less explicit and less individualistic than similar choices made in a modern economy. Hence, prior to market capitalism, an area of such intense economic importance as the division of labour was governed by social considerations which were not primarily economic. 'The division of labor, a phenomenon as old as society, springs from differences inherent in the facts of sex, geography, and individual endowment . . .' (*GT*, p. 44). In marked contrast, the division of labour generated by capitalism is much more intense and results in the fragmentation of occupations and functions. This division of labour is based less on general human differences than on the purely economic dictates of price and cost calculation. In the capitalist economic system, here as elsewhere economic calculation becomes the predominant consideration in organizing social behaviour.

This points up the disembedded character of market capitalist economy, and the contrast of the previous social economic pattern could hardly be more marked. The autonomy and marked visibility of the market economy, witness especially its celebrated self-regulating character, indicate the separation of economic activity and relations from other social activities and relations. 'It is only when production activities become divorced from activities expressing social obligation that production becomes marked off as a peculiarly economic activity, apart from other activities (as, of course, occurs in market economy)' (*TPE*, p. 72; emphasis omitted). It is only with this separation that the economic system can be conceived as having its own laws, its own momentum, and its own self-regulating character.

> It was characteristic of the economic system of the nineteenth century that it was institutionally distinct from the rest of society. In a market economy, the production and distribution of material goods is carried on through a self-regulating system of markets, governed by laws of its own, the so-called laws of supply and demand, motivated in the last resort by two simple incentives, fear of hunger and hope of gain. This institutional arrangement is thus separate from the noneconomic institutions of society: its kinship organization and its political and religious systems. Neither the blood tie, nor legal compulsion, nor religious obligation, nor fealty, nor magic created the sociologically defined situations that insured the participation of individuals in the system. They were, rather, the creation of institutions like private property in the

means of production and the wage system operating on purely economic incentives.

With this state of affairs we are, of course, fairly conversant – livelihood is secured primarily by economic institutions that are activated through economic motives and governed by economic laws. Institutions, motives, and laws are specifically economic. The whole system can be imagined as working without the conscious intervention of human authority, state, or government. No motives other than those of preservation from hunger and of legitimate gain need be invoked, no legal requirement other than protection of property and enforcement of contract is necessary . . . (*LM*, pp. 47–8)

In the history of ideas, the commercial economy with its own momentum or laws of development emerged in England in the seventeenth century and carried the field toward the end of the eighteenth century under the masterful synthesis of Adam Smith. Smith's followers, notably Malthus and Ricardo, took economic ideology a further step and established the control of society by the market economy. For example, consider Malthus on the exercise of procreation, certainly the most basic of all human social relations and functions. For Malthus the right to engage in this human activity is to be determined by one's position in the market. Neither a man nor his children have a right to subsistence unless his labour will fairly purchase it in the market. Malthus refers to this explicitly as a law of nature, which society cannot abrogate without dire consequences. This is in sharp contrast to the traditional economy in which, short of general famine, belonging to the group guarantees the individual his subsistence. Probably, in these earlier societies the right to procreate was limited by other social mechanisms, but in any event it was not read back from the exchange process as in Malthus. In Malthus, then, econocentrism reigns supreme: the locus of meaning is the market economy. Economic function and success dictate social status rather than social status dictating economic position.

The notion of the embedded economy makes it clear that institutions which are now intensely economic, in both the substantive and calculative sense, may have been mixed or decidedly non-economic in their original social position. Their religious, social, or political function may have been predominant. This is true of the market elements which had mixed origins and functions. The discussion also indicates that the economic system is not necessarily one interconnected whole as the notion of the inseparable unity of the market elements implies. The modern economy is such a comprehensive system and we are prone to look everywhere for an economic system in this sense. Where exchange exists in premodern society, it is not unusual to find separate spheres of exchange so that there is one kind of exchange and money appropriate to food, another for ceremonial objects, another for aristocratic consumption, etc.

Moreover, as Dalton has pointed out (*TPE*, pp. 66–71), the various factors engaged in production in premodern economies may be allocated through entirely different institutional channels. The land involved in the production of a particular item may be allocated through one set of social relationships and the labour involved through an entirely different set of relationships. Labour in the production of one item may be allocated differently from the labour involved in producing something else. Various economic activities, since they are not controlled by specifically economic motivations, need not be controlled by a set of interdependent economic relations.

The discussion of embedded economies also indicates that there is a contradiction between the individualism inherent in the market exchange economy and solidarity or strong community relations. Polanyi pointed this out in his discussion of the behavioural motif necessary for the operation of a market economy.

> In order for exchange to be integrative the behavior of the partners must be oriented on producing a price that is as favorable to each partner as he can make it. . . . [E]xchange at fluctuating prices aims at a gain that can be attained only by an attitude involving a distinctive antagonistic relationship between the partners. The element of antagonism, however diluted, that accompanies this variant of exchange is ineradicable. No community intent on protecting the fount of solidarity between its members can allow latent hostility to develop around a matter as vital to physical existence and, therefore, capable of arousing as intense anxieties as food. Hence the universal banning of transactions of a gainful nature in regard to food and foodstuffs in primitive and archaic society. (*PAME*, p. 155)

Sahlins also emphasizes the sensitivity of food in primitive societies and notes that food is often separate from other commodities in the social system (see *SAE*, p. 215ff). For this reason food is very often a separate sphere of exchange. In late medieval England there were extensive regulations by the Crown on matters dealing with food. This too reflects the sensitivity of food in the social system. To take one other example, although the Romans in general tended to give free reign to private contracts, they restricted these contracts with respect to land and food resources.

Such strictures on exchange of commodities for gain, especially those as sensitive as food, point up an established principle of distribution in primitive societies. 'Not to allow anybody reason for jealousy is, indeed, an accepted principle of ceremonial distribution . . .' (*GT*, p. 47). From the ethnographic record it appears that anywhere group identity or community is strong, there is likely to exist very definite institutional mechanisms to suppress jealousy and envy. Clearly, there is some conflict between the individualism and self-gain of the market and the solidarity or social responsibility which is so evident in premodern society. I shall return to such concerns in Chapter 4, but I shall first pause to elaborate upon these institutional concepts by considering the work of Marshall Sahlins.

SAHLINS ON PRIMITIVE ECONOMIES

The type of institutional analysis under discussion is exemplified by Marshall Sahlins' work on primitive economies. He utilizes a wide array of empirical studies in considering the central questions of institutional analysis. The primitive economy is to be understood as the institutionalization of the provisioning function by domestic groups and kinship relations in a society which lacks a state in the sense of an organization which holds a monopoly on the legitimate employment of force. '"[P]rimitive" shall refer to cultures lacking a political state, and it applies only insofar as economy and social relations have not been modified by the historic penetration of states.' (*SAE*, p. 188). As is explained below, the absence of a state to secure peace and order is a fact of major significance to the primitive economy. First, however, I wish to consider the general image of the primitive economy and the spectrum of reciprocities that Sahlins develops.

The Image of the Primitive Economy

One thing that Sahlins' work, and institutional analysis in general, achieve is to correct the common impression that the primitive economy is poverty-ridden, existing precariously on the subsistence margin. This is not an altogether inaccurate image, but it is so in important respects which could lead to the neglect of the very lessons that modern man can learn from the study of primitive economies. These lessons largely lie in the manner by which the primitive society achieved a measure of stability and security despite the absence of a state and the apparent proximity to the subsistence margin.

Sahlins objects to the common view that 'the specter of starvation stalks the stalker. . . . His technical incompetence is said to enjoin continuous work just to survive, affording him neither respite nor surplus, hence not even the "leisure" to "build culture" . . .' (*SAE*, p. 1). The sources of this image are, first, ethnocentrism, especially of the bourgeois variety. In the market mentality, human wants for things are insatiable and scarcity is inevitable even in the context of the vast material means available to modern industrial society. How much more forceful then must scarcity be for primitive society with its much more limited wherewithal. By simple extrapolation, the formalist eclipse of institutional analysis fatally prejudges the investigation of the primitive economy and inhibits empirical analysis of its concrete ends in relation to its means.

Another source of the common image of primitive society is the methodological necessity of relying for data upon extant remnants of hunters and gatherers. In part, this permits further and very naive cultural ethnocentrism. The hunters are seen living in ways unthinkable to the European mind and eating things unpalatable to the European taste, and it is assumed they do so out of dire necessity. A more serious difficulty of this methodological necessity is that the remnant societies are just that, remnants; they are cultural leftovers filling the nooks and crannies of a world which has long since passed them by. They have been pushed aside by progress and enjoy more restricted ecological opportunities than their ancestors; they have also experienced cultural disruption at the hands of European imperialism. That the evidence of their experience nonetheless belies the common image of primitive society is therefore all the more compelling with regard to the conditions of life experienced by their ancestors.

Sahlins presents evidence from a number of empirical studies indicating that 'a kind of material plenty' prevails in the primitive economy. This plenty is not based on having much, but rather upon having, and *wanting*, little. Wanting is limited in quantity and in kind to that which is readily available in the environment, and moderation is institutionally enforced both as to the customary quota of consumption per capita and the number of consumers. Technology is kept very simple and division of labour rudimentary. There is little concern for possessions, even to the extent of being very casual toward the care of such meager possessions as one has. Accumulation of property is not associated with status; it is viewed with disdain and made nearly impossible by the institutionalized liberality of sharing with the less fortunate or less industrious. A thoroughgoing equality prevails in the distribution of property and wealth.

Food and water are objectively scarce and this is undeniably a constraining factor for primitive society. But it is evidently not so direct a constraint as to justify a view that the limited wants stem from the usurpation of all time and attention to the constant struggle for survival. The average work per day in food production is probably between three to five hours per adult worker, and perhaps as many as one-third of adults do not work. The work is not especially arduous, or exhausting, and is not approached as an inherently unpleasant task. Little or no attention is devoted to storing up food for bad times and much easily gatherable food is left to rot ungathered.

The nature of the ecological constraint is indirect; it lies in the cultural adaptation to the limited subsistence base. The central feature of this adaptation is *mobility*. 'Of the hunter it is truly said that wealth is a burden. In his condition of life, goods can become "grievously oppressive". . . . Mobility and property are in contradiction' (*SAE*, pp. 11–12). An advantageous production relation to the environment is maintained by movement and movement precludes much in the way of artifactual accumulation. Not surprisingly, there is a disinterest in making tools, ornaments, clothing, etc. beyond what is necessary; duplication of things is generally avoided; small things are preferred to larger; and even the keeping of food stores is limited. Mobility is also the operant factor behind draconian measures (infanticide and senilicide) to control population. It is the difficulty of moving the young and the old that is significant, not that food is unavailable for them.

One might respond that the movement is so time-consuming as to leave no time for other concerns, but even this is wide of the mark. The travel is anything but frenetic, it is instead rather lazy, pleasant, and unhurried. There is time available to make things, but the sheer factor of mobility militates against doing so because the things would be more burdensome to move than productive of comfort. There is freedom in mobility and there is freedom in not being enslaved by the characteristic desires of bourgeois civilization.

There is evidence that primitive man is aware of this natural contract. Modern hunters and gatherers, surrounded by cultivators, often refuse to take up agriculture themselves on the grounds that it would involve too much hard work. At the very least, it must be admitted that it is the force of ethnocentrism that makes one see only irrationality and ignorance in the primitive disdain for agricultural work or any work beyond necessity, prodigality in eating up foodstuffs, or lack of foresight in not storing food. Given the scarcity born of insatiability that modern man presumes, this judgment has some force. But take away the market mentality and the possibility must be admitted that the primitive mentality is a reasonable confidence resulting from an experience of successful environmental adaptation.

> Speaking to unique developments of the market economy, to its institutionalization of scarcity, Karl Polanyi said that our "animal dependence on food has been bared and the naked fear of starvation permitted to run loose. Our humiliating enslavement to the material, which all human culture is designed to mitigate, was deliberately made more vigorous." (*PAME*, p. 72) But our problems are not theirs, the hunters and gatherers. Rather, a pristine affluence colors their economic arrangements, a trust in the abundance of nature's resources rather than despair at the inadequacy of human means. My point is that otherwise curious heathen devices become understandable by the people's confidence, a confidence which is the reasonable human attribute of a generally successful economy. (*SAE*, pp. 28–9)

It is worth stressing that the point is not to deny the constraints imposed upon primitive economies by their undeniable condition of absolute poverty, but instead to focus on their accommodation to these constraints. Through institutional analysis it is possible to understand this accommodation and learn from it. It is significant, for example, that primitive man approached affluence through a path of limiting wants, very much in contrast to the modern path of ever expanding production in the service of unlimited wants. Insatiability is a cultural propensity rather than a natural one. Scarcity is not a technical condition but a state of mind, a culturally relative mentality rather than a natural fact of life. Acquisitiveness need not be institutionally permitted much less legitimated and encouraged. The institutionally sanctioned limitation of wants is an alternative to 'more'.

In the same vein, it is notable that the limitation of wants is not a practice steeped in a spirit of ascetism and denial. It is habitual, a part of the routine of everyday life as shaped by the institutional adaptation to the ecological context. The spirit of self-denial does not arise in the individual's acceptance of the conditions of his existence.

At any rate, a common feature of primitive economies is underproduction in the sense of producing less than their resources make possible. This condition is not limited to hunting and gathering economies. 'The main run of [primitive economies], agricultural as well as preagricultural, seem not to realize their own economic capacities. Labour power is underused, technological means are not fully engaged, natural resources are left untapped' (*SAE*, p. 41). The attitude toward the maintenance and management of property is casual, even indifferent. Population density relative to ecological carrying capacity is far below technical limits. Incidentally, this does not mean that explanations of social change based on population pressures are necessarily invalid because population would press not on the technical limits of production but on these limits mediated by the social organization. It does mean, though, that any such explanations which neglect institutional analysis should be viewed askance.

The underuse of labour power in primitive economies is even clearer than that of capital and natural resources. The substantial leisure time and leisurely pacing of work has already been noted. The division of labour by sex and age often means that a large share of the available labour force, technically speaking, is not utilized at all or only infrequently. This should not be taken as a resurrection of the jingoistic myth of the indolent savage. It is only to say that motivation to work in primitive economies is not constant, the work is not usually arduous and protracted, and some people work a lot more than others.

An additional consideration is the large variation in production among households in primitive economies. A substantial percentage of households fail to produce their own subsistence and must be supported by interhousehold transfers.

Sahlins goes on to argue that primitive underproduction is explicable by the nature of the household economy or domestic mode of production.

> Structurally, "the economy" does not exist. Rather than a distinct and specialized organization, "economy" is something that generalized social groups and relations, notably kinship groups and relations, *do*. Economy is rather a function of the society than a structure, for the armature of the economic process is provided by groups classically conceived "noneconomic." In particular, production is instituted by domestic groups, these ordinarily ordered as families of one kind or another. The household is to the tribal economy as the manor to the medieval economy or the corporation to modern capitalism: each is the dominant production-institution of its time. Each represents, moreover, a determinate mode of production, with an appropriate technology and division of labor, a characteristic economic objective or finality, specific forms of property, definite social and exchange relations between producing units – and contradictions all its own. In brief, to explain the observed disposition toward underproduction in the primitive economies, I would reconstruct the "independent domestic economy" . . . (*SAE*, p. 76)

The household in the primitive economy is in charge of production, not indirectly as in sovereignty exercised through product and factor markets, but directly because it is the seat of the actual process of production. The principal decisions of production are domestic decisions. Labour allocation and economic objectives are determined in the household and land use is apportioned on a household basis. Household relations, between spouses and parents and children, and kinship relations among households, are the relations of production. Production is carried out by the household and geared to its customary requirements.

This domestic mode of production restricts production in several ways. Specialization of labour is very limited, being principally the division of labour by sex and age. Most tools are simple, small scale, and, along with the skills necessary to use them, within the reach of all household groups. Productive processes are unitary not fragmented, and the same individual can carry out the whole procedure from extraction through to fabrication. Limited division of labour and exchange operate to limit wants because people must rely upon what they can produce for themselves. The greater productive ability of the more efficient minority tends to be underexploited, since output above the social norm must either be shared if kinship relations are strong or serves as an invitation to violence if these relations are weak (*SAE*, p. 88). The predominant economic objective is livelihood, to produce enough to meet customary requirements. The domestic mode of production contains an inherent bias against production of a surplus.

There is a special character to the unintensive pattern of land use. The tendency toward household self-sufficiency and limited interhousehold division of labour tilts primitive society toward household autonomy and anarchy. Villages and banks tend to be small, and if growing, to break up into factions and disperse over this or that conflict. Spatial dispersion, given the absence of a state with a monopoly on force, may be a method of keeping the peace. Conflict over resources is avoided by maintaining utilization well below its technical limits.

Underproduction is not, however, the whole picture since the domestic mode of production does not comprise the whole of primitive society. Although there is no state in the sense of a monopoly on force, there is a polity and political relations. Indeed, it seems that there must be or primitive society could not survive because the tendency toward splintering and the anti-surplus principle of the household economy make no provision for disaster, defence, or public economy of any kind. The political relations are those of kinship and leadership and these operate to overcome, in part, the resistance to production of the household economy. One way the kinship system operates to do this has already been noted in the variation of production among households, some of which do not produce their own subsistence. Other households are induced to produce beyond their own requirements in order to share with the less productive. Where chieftainship exists, the obligation to tithe to the chief induces households to labour beyond their own requirements; the chief's household must do likewise if he is to practice the generosity incumbent upon his status. Short of chieftainship proper, there is usually a 'big man' system of some sort and the big man gains his status by being able to provide lavish feasts or give aid when it is needed. Big men are not kings, i.e. hereditary nobility with a monopoly on force; they are merely superior kinsmen and their superiority is based on doing better than others and on their ability to practise generosity. This not only stimulates production in the households of big men and chiefs but also in those of their followers. These political relations also operate to intensify land use by overcoming, in part, the tendency toward dispersion. Interhousehold kinship provides for peaceable relations in the absence of a state with a monopoly on force.

The polity can overcome to some degree the tendency toward underproduction. That primitive societies endure attests to this but that they remain underproductive attests to the fact that there are limits on the political intensification of production. There is a permanent tension between the domestic and public economies. 'The household is never entirely submerged in the larger community, nor are domestic ties ever free from conflict with wider kin relationships. This is a permanent contradiction of primitive society and economy' (*SAE*, p. 124). Various political arrangements and individual personalities have differential effects on economic production and much depends on the strength and extent of kinship relations. Without a state, there are limits to the political intensification of production, and these limits represent the boundaries of primitive society itself. The importance of the state in economic evolution and in the current context of economic development is made clear here, as is Marx's dictum that force is the midwife of every old society pregnant with the new. The state should likewise be expected to be the key in the transition to capitalism, about which Polanyi had much to say, as I point out in the next chapter.

That primitive society constrains production below what it could be lends substance to a major theme of Polanyi's work, the embedded economy. Society here dictates economy, rather than the reverse as in market capitalism where everything in the social fabric is geared to maximum production. The image of primitive economy should be revised to include attention to its concrete institutional reality. It would seem that there is little or no surplus *produced*, it is rather left unproduced, perhaps as a margin of safety due to the potentially precarious proximity to the subsistence margin. At any rate, primitive society does encapsulate its economy, and it is bent on sufficiency and livelihood rather than efficiency and maximization.

Reciprocity and Primitive Exchange

In discussing integrative mechanisms, though citing his debt to his mentor, Polanyi, Sahlins collapses the latter's threefold scheme of reciprocity, redistribution, and market exchange into a twofold division by subsuming exchange under reciprocity. He also notes that redistribution is in essence a system of reciprocities but insists separate classification should be maintained nonetheless due to their very different social organizations: reciprocity implies a *between* relation of distinct socioeconomic interests whereas redistribution implies a *within* relation of a unified collectivity (*SAE*, p. 188–9). There is some hint along these lines in Polanyi's work, as when he notes that Aristotle treated exchange as part of reciprocity behaviour, which 'might be called reciprocity on the square' (*PAME*, p. 110). But the point seems to be that this balanced transacting was not market exchange because the latter is by definition (Polanyi's) disembedded. Polanyi also mentions the subordination of redistribution and exchange to reciprocity in practice (*PAME*, p. 153), but again he appears to exclude market exchange.

I should record that I am not entirely comfortable with Sahlins' subsumption of exchange into reciprocity. His point is well taken that since transactions empirically often fall in between the typologies of reciprocity and market exchange, a continuum approach has merit (*SAE*, p. 196). However, treating market exchange as a form of reciprocity does reduce the *visibility* of Polanyi's major typological factor, the disembedded character of the former. If Polanyi is right, the difference in substance if not in form of social organization is at least as great between market exchange and reciprocity as between the latter and redistribution. This is not to say that Sahlins loses sight of the embeddedness factor; he does not, but only that he renders it less obvious. This would seem to make it easier to neglect the concrete institutional differences between market exchange and reciprocity.

Sahlins' spectrum of reciprocities extends from freely given assistance, generalized reciprocity, at one end to self-interested seizure by force or chicane, negative reciprocity, at the other.[6] *Generalized reciprocity* is 'putatively altruistic' and indicated in the ethnographic record by such terms as sharing, generosity, help, free gift, or hospitality. It occurs also where the obligation is more formalized such as in kinship dues or chiefly dues. The material aspect of the transaction is dominated by the social relations which obtain. The key element seems to be the absence of direct and immediate reciprocation. The reciprocation is indefinite as to worth and timing and it is unseemly to expect equal and immediate return. A good operational indicator of generalized reciprocity is a sustained one-way flow.

In the middle of the spectrum is *balanced reciprocity* which involves direct exchange between socioeconomic interests which are more distinct and less closely related interpersonally than in generalized reciprocal transactions. Here the indicative terms in the ethnographic record are gift-exchange, payments, or trade. Reciprocation is here expected to be of customarily equivalent worth and made without delay or at least within a finite and narrow period. The material aspect of the transaction is greater relative to the social, and the social relations are not close enough to sustain a one-way flow.

The unsociable extreme, *negative reciprocity*, involves the attempt of opposed and impersonal interests to get something for nothing, to secure the unearned increment. The following ethnographic terms are indicative of negative reciprocity: haggling, barter, gambling, chicanery, or theft. The more sociable degree of negative reciprocity is haggling to secure the most favourable terms that the traffic will bear. One-way flows are possible here depending on the degree of countervailing power or chicanery.

The question arises as to the position on the spectrum of market exchange. Clearly, it would fall somewhere along the segment from balanced to negative reciprocity. Ideally, it would fall on or near balanced reciprocity if exchange is strictly voluntary, information available to all parties, etc. Competitive market forces leading to exchange at necessary supply price would bring about this result. Where competition among buyers or among sellers is lax, market exchange tilts toward the negative reciprocity pole. Given the Marxist and Veblenian insistence on the predatory, exploitative character of market capitalism, it would seem that negative reciprocity is the typical individual goal. Veblen's persistent use of the term *sharp practice* no doubt reflects his attention to the ethnographic record where the term abounds to describe behaviour dedicated to securing what Sahlins terms negative reciprocity. Marx's emphasis on the illusory character of the voluntary exchange model at least between capital and labour points in the same direction.

Sahlins goes on to consider social factors that orient transactions to one or another position on the spectrum of reciprocities. Kinship rank usually encourages generalized reciprocity, not only in tributes to big men or chiefs but also in the almost universal obligation for the leaders to practise generosity towards their followers. The economic inequality found in medieval feudalism is not common in primitive societies where 'social inequality is more the organization of economic equality' due to the generosity of primitive paternalism (*SAE*, p. 205). Differences in wealth in primitive society encourage generalized reciprocity: 'given some social bond between those who exchange, differences in fortune between them compel a more altruistic (generalized) transaction than is otherwise appropriate' (*SAE*, p. 211). Food is a particularly revealing category in social organization and generalized reciprocity extends further in food transactions than in other things.

Social or kinship distance, together with the closely related consideration of spatial proximity, seem to be the most important variables in the social structure in the determination of the sort of reciprocity that prevails. Close relatives living together in a household clearly require generalized reciprocity. Generalized reciprocity usually extends to the village level in primitive societies but probably not all the way to the tribal level. Balanced reciprocity is likely to prevail in the intratribal sector beyond the village economy.

In the intertribal sector, negative reciprocity is a distinct possibility. Tribal morality permits cheating or robbing the enemy or stranger and this is likely to apply to anyone who may be classed as 'them, not us', i.e. non-kin. This should come as no surprise to historians of economic thought who are familiar with the evolution of doctrine concerning usury. The taking of interest from foreigners was seldom castigated even when the condemnation of usury was at its strongest. Balanced reciprocity may, however, extend into the intertribal sector in the presence of special social arrangements such as trade partnerships. By such arrangements, negative reciprocity is institutionally suppressed in the interest of maintaining amicable relations. Indeed, balanced reciprocity is the 'classic vehicle of peace and alliance contracts', demonstrating on both sides 'some renunciation of hostile intent or indifference in favour of mutuality' (*SAE*, p. 220). Such reciprocation can thus establish relations between tribes serving, to use Alvin Gouldner's term, as a 'starting mechanism'.[7] Trade partnerships are usually insulated social relations between individuals of different tribes. In time, intermarriage may occur and partnerships evolve into kinship ties.

To understand the diplomatic importance of primitive trade and reciprocity, it is necessary to realize the sociological reality of the Hobbesian chaos. This underlying reality exists even in modern political systems where it is explicitly suppressed, but it must be much clearer in primitive society where it is much nearer the social surface. Recall that the indicative condition here is the absence of a state and the kind of law associated with the political state, so that individuals and groups of necessity take the law, so to speak, into their own force-wielding hands. The gift, the process of reciprocation, can then be seen, as Marcel Mauss suggests, as a primitive social contract to overcome extreme fear and hostility by equally extreme generosity. To reject reciprocity, whether by refusing to give, to receive, or to reciprocate, is tantamount to a declaration of hostile intent. The delicacy and potential explosiveness of intertribal trade is then obvious, as Claude Lévi-Strauss notes: 'Exchanges are peacefully resolved wars, and wars are the result of unsuccessful transactions' (*SAE*, p. 302). Primitive trade is a process of diplomacy and exchange rates are akin to peace treaties. The biting if humorous social commentary of Walter Goldschmidt's observation on an American primitive society is therefore appreciable: '"While trading, Indians won't hand a foreigner both the bow and arrows at the same time"' (*SAE*, p. 302n).

Understanding of a familiar point is hereby deepened: 'every exchange, as it embodies some coefficient of sociability, cannot be understood in its material terms apart from its social terms' (*SAE*, p. 183). 'A material transaction is usually a momentary episode in a continuous social relation [and] the social relation exerts governance: the flow of goods is constrained by, is part of, a status etiquette' (*SAE*, pp. 185–6). The economy, or, in this case, exchange, which appears to be the economy to the catallactics purview, is embedded in society. The parenthetical note is necessary because exchange and production are not intimately connected: 'the place of transaction in the total economy is different: under primitive conditions it is more detached from production' (*SAE*, p. 187). Since exchange is not the predominant form of integration, it does not predominate over production and resource allocation – nor for that matter over distribution.

This brings up another familiar point: if exchange, even of the gainless variety, is peripheral economically, then how much more so must be gainful exchange, the motive peculiarly relevant to the market economy. Once again, this is not to say that selfishness is absent, only that it is checked by moral obligations in the context of the high 'publicity of primitive life'. Meanness is generally the most vilified vice and generosity the highest virtue. One needs a reputation for generosity if for no other reason than the possibility that one may someday be dependent on the generosity of others. Great lengths are taken to avoid generating envy of one's possessions and gift-giving, both compulsorily structured and spontaneous, is an endless preoccupation. 'The *objective* of gathering wealth, indeed, is often that of giving it away' (*SAE*, p. 123). More overt sanctions are present in the ethnographic record, e.g. kin have been known to destroy the possessions of those who are excessively avaricious. Big men or chiefs who despite the premium placed on their generosity, are persistently greedy and exploitative have been put to death by their people.

The background to such behaviour has already been noted, the domestic mode's tendency toward dispersion and the threat of the Hobbesian war of all against all. Just how real is this underlying sociology is indicated by the effects on reciprocity of a crisis situation, such as natural disaster or war mobilization. Hard times may pull all together and extend reciprocity and generosity, at least for a time. But, depending on the strength of solidarity as opposed to the scale and duration of the disaster, a contrary movement may occur and cooperation decline.

> Probably every primitive organization has its breaking-point, or at least its turning-point. Everyone might see the time when cooperation is overwhelmed by the scale of the disaster and chicanery becomes the order of the day. The range of assistance contracts progressively to the family level; perhaps even these bonds dissolve and, washed away, reveal an inhuman, yet most human, self-interest. Moreover, by the same measure that the circle of charity is compressed that of "negative reciprocity" is potentially expanded. People who helped each other in normal times and through the first stages of disaster display now indifference to each others' plight, if they do not exacerbate a mutual downfall by guile, haggle, and theft. Put another way, the whole sectoral scheme of reciprocities is altered, compressed: sharing is confined to the innermost sphere of solidarity and all else is devil take the hindmost. (*SAE*, p. 214)

Consider, finally, the case of the Southeast Asian primitive communities which exist as hinterlands engaged in petty market trade to more advanced cultural centres. When the primitives trade rice for cash, iron goods, or prestige items, their social economy dramatically changes. Minimally, households must be permitted to accumulate rather than share their surplus rice production; therefore, household production variations are not liquidated in the distribution sphere. The intensity of village sharing lessens and balanced reciprocity prevails in interhousehold relations because kinship ties are weakened and solidary relations are compressed to the household level. Prestige is shifted to accumulation of objects and away from generosity. Community structure is fragmented and political leadership and followership declines.

In reading of this example, I was struck by the similarity of effects between contact with the market economy and natural or military disaster. Much is already known along these lines from the literature on developing countries with respect to the cultural disruption of Western imperialism and colonialism. Much less is known or even acknowledged concerning the effects of the market economy on community, society, polity, and culture *within* the Western countries themselves. This problem of lives and livelihood was the characteristic concern of Polanyi's work.

4 The Political Economy of Market Capitalism

As I indicated above, there is a further and most important dimension to Polanyi's concern than the methodological problems of economic anthropology, economic history, and comparative economic systems. The economistic conception lies at the root of a paralytic *gestalt* which is fixated on the market form of economic organization. This institutional fixation does more than break down what should be the continuity between the analyses of past economies and comparative economic systems. It so delimits the vision of economic analysis that alternative institutional forms are not visible. This astigmatism similarly cripples the economist's approach to public policy and social reform with the result that basic institutional change is unimaginable.

Moreover, the problem in question is not limited even to economic theory in general because the economistic *gesalt* is not limited to economists. It shapes social consciousness in general and can be easily found in the utterances of labour leaders, business executives, governmental officials, and non-economist academicians. Indeed, as I argue in this chapter, the market society which is required for the operation of a self-regulating market economy is a society in which economic calculus colours all walks of life. It is an *econocentric* society, one in which economic desiderata form the central locus of meaning permeating all social activity. The practical significance of the market myth is therefore of much greater importance than the debilitation of the thinking of members of the economics profession. The stress on the methodology and perspective of economists is still important, however, because there is found the logical expression of economistic institutions. Moreover, economists comprise the group which can most advantageously lead the reinterpretation of economy and society. In an econocentric society, the views of economists are important in the trend of public opinion.

This chapter is concerned with the political economy of market capitalism. It discusses, first, the character and collapse of the nineteenth-century social economy. In the second and third sections, I elaborate Polanyi's analysis of this character and collapse. In the final section, I present an explanation of social evolution in the twentieth century based upon Polanyi's analysis of market capitalism.

THE CHARACTER AND COLLAPSE OF THE NINETEENTH-CENTURY SOCIAL ECONOMY

Polanyi began *The Great Transformation* with a discussion of the four principal institutions of the nineteenth-century social order. He classified these institutions as to their economic or political and national or international characters. The four were the balance-of-power system, political and international; the gold standard, economic and international; the liberal state, political and national; and the self-regulating market economy, economic and national. These institutions, significantly, sustained the century of peace between the Napoleonic war and World War I. In Polanyi's view, of these four institutions, the decisive one was the self-regulating market: 'It was this innovation which gave rise to a specific civilization' (*GT*, p. 3). It was, he felt, the economic system which underwrote the 'pragmatic pacifism' by creating a 'peace interest'. The world-wide financial interests, the movers of *haute finance*, had a financial interest in averting world war, notwithstanding their interests in a series of colonial wars which were limited in extent and specific in purpose.

It follows that the breakdown of the nineteenth-century institutional pattern was based on the collapse of the self-regulating market. From the turn of the twentieth century onward, the international economic system was in process of dissolution as was the political system based upon it. The breakdown of the gold standard in the early 1930s was the symbolic demise of one age and the harbinger of the coming transformation of civilization. This was Polanyi's thesis in *The Great Transformation*: 'the origins of the cataclysm [of the 1920s and 1930s] lay in the utopian endeavour of economic liberalism to set up a self-regulating market system' (*GT*, p. 29). The transformation thereafter, the emergence of the corporate–welfare state, was to Polanyi a related problem of political economy. The breakdown of the nineteenth century stemmed from the belief in the self-regulating market and the conception of the state-as-necessary-evil. Understanding of the breakdown of the nineteenth century is critical to the corporate–welfare state because the latter is a response to the same institutional problems as those which toppled the nineteenth-century dream. These institutional problems cluster around Polanyi's characteristic lives and livelihood problem. Any mechanism of economic integration requires a correspondent social system which supports it and surrounds it with meaning. It is in the market society required for the functioning of a market economy that one finds many of the characteristic stresses and strains of market capitalism.

The self-regulating economy is an economy guided by the variations in relative prices. The business firm must be able to buy, with considerable stability and predictability, the factors of production which it transforms and sells for its income. Short of this, the risk attendant to the construction and operation of a machine-intensive plant would be too great (*GT*, p. 41). Saddled with such a plant, the firm bears considerable fixed or overhead costs which must be met over the short term irrespective of the level of output. If raw materials and labour supplies cannot be confidently expected to be available, such overhead costs would prevent large-scale, machine production. The predictable availability of these supplies requires that factor owners be dependent upon market exchange for their livelihood, i.e. hunger and similar needs must elicit the response on the part of the individual to earn an income (*PAME*, p. 64). This response is a matter of socialization in a general sense, but most important is the crude cudgel of economic necessity. The creation of the home market for substantive subistence requirements involved the dissolution of traditional social relationships and patterns of provisioning. The domestic mode of production, largely self-sufficient production for direct use, was destroyed and commodity production, production for exchange, took its place. 'No market economy was conceivable that did not include a market for labour; but to establish such a market, especially in England's rural civilization, implied no less than the wholesale destruction of the traditional fabric of society' (*GT*, p. 77). The feudal serfs first became independent peasant farmers, later their land tenure was dissolved and they became the urban proletariat of necessity selling their labour power on the market. In the same process, land too became alienable, i.e. saleable on the market.

Thus, the industrialist's markets were secured in a double sense. First, as mentioned, the factors of production were for sale on the market, reliably so because their owners were dependent on the market to earn an income with which to provision their substantive requirements. Second, the industrialist secured a reliable market for his output, the effective demand to fulfil these same requirements. I am not, of course, contending that market capitalism is stable in the sense of the modern concern for economic stabilization. This social economy is patently instable in the sense of periodic fluctuations and business risk is inherently present. But it is one thing for an industrialist to face higher or lower prices than he expects but quite another for the industrialists as a whole to face labourers or raw materials suppliers who produce their own subsistence and market only a surplus not related to their self-sufficiency. Without their direct production to meet their requirements, labourers must sell their labour power to someone and buy commodities to meet their needs from someone (*PAME*, p. 57). Land ownership, once land was marketable, became capitalized and raw materials supply became a production goods industry.

The market society necessary for the operation of a market economy is largely subservient to the economy.

> [O]nce man's everyday activities have been organized through markets of various kinds, based on profit motives, determined by competitive attitudes, and governed by a utilitarian value scale, his society becomes an organism that is, in all essential regards, subservient to gainful purposes. Having thus absolutized the motive of economic gain in practice, he loses the capacity of mentally relativizing it again. His imagination is bounded by stultifying limits. The very word *economy* evokes in him not the picture of man's livelihood and the technology that helps to secure it, but recalls instead a set of particular motives, peculiar attitudes, and highly specific purposes, all of which he is used to calling *economic*. . . . (*LM*, p. xlvi)

I return to the dominance of the economy over society in the remaining sections of this chapter. First, however, I review Polanyi's discussion of the history of markets and the origin of the market economy.

Polanyi's universal economic history taught him that the market, though a very old institution, had never been, before the modern era, the central loci of socioeconomic organization, and it was seldom even an important institution.

> In spite of the chorus of academic incantations so persistent in the nineteenth century, gain and profit made on exchange never before played an important part in human economy. Though the institution of the market was fairly common since the later Stone Age, its role was no more than incidental to economic life. (*GT*, p. 43)

Market exchange in pre-capitalist economic formations was usually limited to transactions between different communities and was uncommon in the social relationships within a given community (*LM*, p. 78). Such long-distance trade was usually limited to luxury and non-essential articles, and was relatively unimportant in the everyday life of common citizens because their substantive subsistence requirements were not involved.

Included in the market myth is the conviction that the market institution is somehow supremely consonant with human nature and its characteristic motivations – Adam Smith's inveterate 'propensity to truck, barter, and exchange'. This bias, crudely but not inaccurately rendered, reads from history that the market institution is ubiquitous, and will provide a stable, secure, efficient, and just integration of economic activity unless it is suppressed or distorted by the workings of sinister or ignorant political forces. Without such political machinations, the market economy will inevitably arise. In view of this bias, Polanyi took great pains to challenge the ubiquity of the market institution in its modern sense, and to stress the peculiar historical circumstances from which the self-regulating market economy emerged.

Viewed through the eyes of the economistic fallacy, market exchange appears ubiquitous. Division of labour is present in antiquity and how could it be present without exchange of products? Moreover, there is evidence of trade, money use, and markets, and for the economistically-minded, these three categories are inseparably united. Polanyi challenged both this inseparable unity and the presence of markets in the modern sense. On the latter, he noted that archaeology can provide evidence that markets existed in the sense of *places* where people met and exchanged goods. But it is much more difficult to determine if a market existed in the sense of a supply–demand–price mechanism (*LM*, p. 124). Yet, in the purview of the economistic fallacy, the presence of market places implies the presence of the supply–demand–price mechanism. Moreover, even in the place sense, markets are historically much younger than trade and money use (*LM*, p. 123).

To counter the claim of ubiquitous market exchange, Polanyi analysed the history of trade, money, and markets – the catallactic triad. He did so in order to repudiate the inseparable unity of the catallactic triad. The importance of this repudiation is easy to understand: if the triad is necessarily unified, then wherever one finds one ingredient of the triad, it can be presumed that the others are also present. To invalidate such a conclusion, Polanyi argued that these three components had different origins, were integrated and functioned differently in different societies in diverse ways, and were not necessarily cohabitous (*LM*, pp. 77–9). Polanyi examines each part of the triad and finds instances in which each existed without the other two, and that each has several different types and functions in society (*LM*, pp. 95–5, 109, 116–17, and 126 ff.). Trade can be divided into gift trade, treaty trade, and market trade (*LM*, pp. 94–5). The first is an instance of reciprocity and the second a matter of diplomacy. Only the third approaches what is meant by trade in the catallactic triad.

On money, Polanyi argues that antiquity had no all-purpose money but different money symbols which were specific in their use (*LM*, p. 98). Different money symbols existed for trade in different aspects or between different social strata (*LM*, p. 117). In the modern view, money serves to enable indirect exchange, i.e. money as a medium of exchange. On this view, the other functions of money, unit of account, means of payment, or store of value, are derivative from the means of exchange function (*LM*, p. 104). Polanyi counters this and contends that the various functions of money had separate origins (*LM*, p. 109). Even the function of payment does not have to exist in tandem with exchange. 'Money is now a means of payment *because* it is a means of exchange. The very notion of the independent origin of payment is lost, and the millenia of human civilization in which payment sprang not from economic transactions, but directly from religious, social, or political obligations, have been forgotten' (*LM*, p. 107). The importance of these distinctions is that 'they explain the functioning of the various money uses in the absence of a market system' (*LM*, p. 116).

Polanyi also found a variety of market types in archaic society. The various types were special purpose in the same way that money objects or trade were (*LM*, ch. 10). The presence of some of the various elements of market exchange does not necessarily mean that a price-making market is in operation. The market elements, institutionally speaking, i.e. a physical site, goods for exchange, a supply crowd, a demand crowd, a customary or legal framework, and equivalencies or rates of exchange can all be present without there also being a supply–demand–price mechanism (*LM*, p. 125). The question arises: without price-making markets, how are relative prices established? The answer is that they may be established by custom, administration, or law: it is the means by which prices are established, and not their mere presence, upon which turns the type of market, trade, or money that exists (*LM*, p. 125). In other words, equivalencies may be established by other social institutions than the market mechanism. For example, 'the proclamation of equivalencies is one of the main functions of the archaic king' (*LM*, p. 74). In the absence of the market mechanism, meetings to exchange goods 'do not establish rates of exchange, but, on the contrary presuppose them' (*LM*, p. 81). Exchange at prices set by custom, treaty, or administration is not market exchange, and the integrative force is supplied, not by the market institution, but by the institutions of custom, diplomacy, or administration.

In denying the inseparable unity of the catallactic triad, Polanyi was leading up to the prevalence of administered trade where economic historians too often see market trade, notably in Archaic Greece, to which Polanyi devoted a large part of *The Livelihood of Man*. He found, in the case of the all-important area of grain, administered or treaty trade. The safety of trade routes and the terms of trade were determined diplomatically (*LM*, p. 205) and secured by military control (*LM*, p. 214). Polanyi quotes from Aristotle's *Rhetoric* to indicate the administrative attitude toward trade. '[I]n regard to food, [the statesman] should know what amount of expenditure is sufficient to support the State; what kind of food is produced at home or can be imported; and what exports and imports are necessary, in order that contracts and agreements can be made with those who can furnish them' (*LM*, p. 206). Clearly the provisioning function is viewed by Aristotle as a matter of administration by public policy. No vision of an automatic economic process is in view. The prevalence of administered trade is also evident in other products, such as timber, bronze, hemp, and wax (*LM*, p. 225). Careful reading of the Athenian administered economy leaves one the impression that mercantilist-type measures were used to control the economy, but that this control was not aimed at securing a favourable trade balance but rather at provisioning the substantive requirements of society.

Economic transactions were constrained by custom and administration and the exchange relationship was not allowed to exist per se, without being embedded in other social relationships. Social solidarity was maintained by measures to preclude exchange as a purely gainful operation. Gainless trade removes the 'invidious element' of gainful exchange and economic transactions are subordinated to the social purpose of provisioning (*LM*, p. 61). The invidious element of wealth was also undermined by the *alien* position of traders in archaic society. Often, the resident alien traders were segregated from the city-state populace. These traders could grow wealthy in the pecuniary sense but they could not buy social or political status with their wealth. For example, the *metic* trader in Athens could not own land or a house. He could not then expend his money on the material things which went along with high social status in Athenian society, e.g. he could not build a mansion, give feasts, or raise horses (*LM*, p. 88). In some trade sectors, there were citizen traders, but they were traders *despite* being citizens; trade was not their occupation by status, i.e. trade was not their proper or honourable pursuit. Such citizen-traders were very lowly regarded (*LM*, p. 192). In *Politics*, Aristotle insisted that some geographical separation of the emporium be maintained, but not so much as to cause inconvenience. He felt that the state could guard against the harmful effects on its citizenry of interacting with traders 'by means of laws regulating which persons are not and which persons are to have intercourse with one another' (*LM*, p. 232).

Polanyi acknowledged that trade and money frequently coexisted with the market elements in archaic society but he denied that they were either unified or had any pronounced tendency toward unification. Specifically, it is sometimes maintained that Roman society was destined to develop into modern capitalism but that this destiny was denied by the decline of the Empire. Something like capitalism was undeniably developing in Rome, and the Romans developed much of the legal framework later to be a cornerstone of modern capitalism. Still, Polanyi maintained, citing Max Weber, that Roman capitalism was altogether different from modern capitalism and displayed no inherent tendency to evolve the traits of the modern form (*LM*, pp. 275–6).

In a similar vein, Polanyi warned against the tendency toward teleological thinking with regard to the origin of market capitalism.

> The temptation, in our own age, to regard the market economy as the natural goal of some three thousand years of Western development is overwhelming. . . . Western thought is almost incapable of conceiving of [market elements] in any manner, except as the small beginnings that eventually grew into the world-encompassing economy of the modern age. Nothing could be more mistaken. Market trade itself, and eventually the modern market economy, were the results, not of a process of growth from small beginnings, but rather of the convergences of originally separate and independent developments that cannot be understood apart from an analysis of the institutional elements that went into their making. (*LM*, p. 125)

This underscores the importance of the formalist eclipse of institutional analysis. The formalist ethnocentrism impairs the ability to recognize that the disparate elements which are fused in the market economy existed for centuries without undergoing such fusion. There is no ineluctable historical force set in motion toward this denouement by their mere coexistence. The logic which inevitably fuses them is hindsight, the familiar categorical misreading of the past discussed in Chapter 2. Market capitalism 'is more than a mere variant of trading. The principle of exchange implied in trade is, under capitalism, put to a wholly different use than acquisition of goods from a distance' (*LM*, p. 124). Market exchange in capitalist society is the predominant social institution. Never before had any or all of the market elements been axial institutions to that degree.

The market elements per se do not imply the inevitable emergence of the market economy, they need not undergo fusion and even if fused, in all their additivity and synergy, they do not per se form a market economy. There is an additional requirement for the emergence of the market economy, and this requirement was met in the nineteenth century, not by ineluctable historical forces, but by *conscious human design*. This additional requirement is the internal, national, or home market, a thing apart from purely local or long-distance, extra-societal markets.

> The step which makes isolated markets [or market elements] into

> a market economy, regulated markets into a self-regulating market, is indeed crucial. The nineteenth century . . . naively imagined that such a development was the natural outcome of the spreading of markets. It was not realized that the gearing of markets into a self-regulating system of tremendous power was not the result of any inherent tendency of markets toward excrescence, but rather the effect of highly artificial stimulants administered to the body social. . . . The limited and unexpansive nature of the market pattern as such, was not recognized . . . . (*GT*, p. 57)

Local trade consists of bulky, perishable, or heavy goods which are not portable and for which a locality is self-sufficient. External trade consists of portable items not available in the importing locale. Both local and external trade are *complementary* and entail no necessary competition. Internal trade is inherently competitive because it involves exchanges among several types of similar goods in a given locale (*GT*, p. 60). Therefore, 'neither long-distance nor local trade was the parent of the internal trade of modern times' (*GT*, p. 63).

What, then, was the seminal fluid which, cast into the womb of market elements, fathered the internal market? There is 'no alternative but to turn for an explanation to the *deus ex machina* of state intervention . . ., [i]nternal trade in Western Europe was actually created by the intervention of the state' (*GT*, p. 63). The first step in this intervention was mercantilism, created by 'deliberate action of the state in the fifteenth and sixteenth centuries [which] foisted the mercantile system on the fiercely protectionist towns and principalities' (*GT*, p. 65). Mercantilism uprooted the several forms of special purpose trading of medieval particularism and cleared the way for an integrated, all-purpose national market. But, mercantilism did not thusly create the self-regulating competitive market economy. By creating the internal market, mercantilism made a degree of competition inevitable, but the traditional regulation or administration of trade prevailed over this new regulatory force.[1] The next step in social history, the creation of one big self-regulating market was not made by mercantilism and 'there was nothing in mercantilism . . . to presage such a development.' Mercantile commercial trade remained embedded in the social fabric and was politically administered (*GT*, pp. 66–7). Mercantilism viewed markets in a way directly contrary to a market economy, as a policy tool of the positive state (*GT*, p. 70). Specifically, mercantilism took the traditional organization of land and labour for granted, and displayed no tendency to remove the protective social fabric from these basic social categories, nor to subject them to the rigours of commercial organization (*GT*, pp. 70–1). In the terminology of the next section, mercantilism engenders neither a disembedded economy nor the fictitious treatment of land and labour as commodities.

Polanyi's point is that the market economy is in no way a natural or spontaneous outgrowth of the human condition. His intent is to repudiate both the classical contention that the market economy is most consonant with natural law and human nature and the evolutionist view of the teleological origin of the market economy. To the contrary, the state intervened to establish the market economy and thereafter continuously endeavoured to maintain it. It is not the *laissez-faire* economy but the reaction *against* it that is spontaneous (*GT*, pp. 140–1 and 149). This spontaneous counteraction, which Polanyi labelled the *protective response*, is considered in detail below in this chapter.

Polanyi's contention that the market economy was instituted via conscious human design is both novel and controversial. He certainly did not mean to say that the idea of the self-regulating market antedated the widespread influence of market forces. 'From the sixteenth century onwards markets were both numerous and important' (*GT*, p. 55). His point was instead that however widespread and numerous, the mere existence of markets does not imply a market economy in the sense of an autonomous, distinctive, and largely self-regulating sphere of human activity. The installation of a market economy thusly conceived required political action. Such action, being intentional, required an ideological directive. This directive was compellingly supplied by the classical economists around the turn of the nineteenth century, during the course of which the market economy in Polanyi's sense was institutionalized.

The basic structure of the classical movement was laid in place by Adam Smith. Consider T. W. Hutchison's reading of the revolutionary character of Smith's work: 'Adam Smith . . . generalized the theory of market self-adjustment as operating effectively, by and large . . . throughout the economic cosmos, domestically and internationally, micro-economically and macro-economically.'[2] Prior to Smith the various markets were not viewed as comprising a self-regulating *system*. Some writers touched upon automaticity in different markets but it was Smith's grand synthesis which articulated the vision of the self-regulating system of markets. The various markets which awaited Smith's classical synthesis are not far removed from Polanyi's separate market elements and types.

The question arises: was Smith merely reflecting, intellectually, those changes which had in reality already occurred? Was classical economics an ad hoc rationalization of an institutional configuration which was already firmly in place? It would seem that the answer must be no if one accepts Polanyi's view of a consciously designed, utopian experiment with a market economy. Notwithstanding the growth of the market forces that had obviously occurred before the classical intellectual expression of the automatic market, Polanyi has strong grounds on which to stand. Hutchison concurs with Polanyi's dates (*PAME*, p. 67): 'The framework of the free-market, free-trade economy [was] established in the 1830s and 1840s.'[3] Benjamin Ward attributes to the 'conservative economic world view' the conviction that 'the thoroughgoing trading society' emerged first in nineteenth-century England and America.[4]

It would seem to be undeniable fact that the *laissez-faire* policy toward the competitive market framework was established in considerable part through the efforts of the classical economists, especially the elder Mill and Ricardo, and that they did so with clarity of intent. Hutchison argues that the

> main meaning and intention of the Millian-Ricardian theories and methods can be found in the nature of the policy conclusions derived from them. Ricardo's policy conclusions, which he went into Parliament to proclaim with all the authority of the new science behind him, followed from, and depended on, with great exactness and rigidity, his "strongly" simplified assumptions or theories. The Millian-Ricardian abstract, deductive method started from starkly unqualified assumptions . . . [that] led immediately and inevitably to sharply *laissez-faire* policy doctrines.[5]

There is also evidence that nineteenth-century scholars were aware of the ideal, experimental character of the market economy. Walter Bagehot observed in 1895 that 'it is difficult for a modern Englishman, to whom "free trade" is an accepted maxim of tedious orthodoxy, to remember sufficiently that a hundred years ago it was a heresy and a paradox. The whole commercial legislation of the world was [then] formed on the doctrines of protection'.[6] Nassau Senior, celebrating the British economic advance, proclaimed in

1851 that this advance 'is a triumph of theory. We are governed by philosophers and political economists'.[7] J. E. Cairnes (1870):

> Great Britain, if not the birth place of Political Economy, has at least been its early home, as well as the scene of the most signal triumphs of its manhood. Every great step in the progress of economic science . . . has been won by English thinkers; and while we have led the van in economic speculation, we have also been the first to apply with boldness our theories to practice. Our foreign trade, our colonial policy, our poor-laws, our fiscal system, each has in turn been reconstructed from the foundation upwards under the inspiration of economic ideas; and the population and the commerce of the country, responding to the impulse given by the new principles operating through these changes, have within a century multiplied themselves manifold. This London, . . . what is it but a mighty monument of economic achievement? – the greatest practical illustration which the world has seen of the potent influence of those principles which it is the business of the political economist to expound?[8]

J. L. Simonde de Sismondi, commenting on Great Britain at mid-century, noted that '[t]his astonishing country . . . seems to be committed to a great experiment for the instruction of the rest of the world . . .'.[9] The pre-eminence of the economy and the ideal, grand design of classicism shows clearly through these quotations.

Polanyi's emphasis on the nineteenth-century institutional reconstruction and Hutchison's emphasis on Smith's decisive synthesis may be a bit misleading though substantially true. The decisive break with the traditional economic mentality may have occurred in the seventeenth century.[10] In that century an intense ideological struggle was waged over the place of economy in British society. The growing importance of market forces created a situation in which human lives were being influenced by impersonal and anonymous, poorly understood and literally unimaginable forces. The result was a *cultural* crisis which set men in search of a new interpretive reality. The traditional view with its subordination of economy to society, manifested in this instance by the moral economy administered by the British crown and aristocracy, was shaken to its foundations and eventually replaced by the market mentality. This new mentality did not immediately rise to dominate economic thought; its ultimate victory awaited the bold pen of

Adam Smith. Nonetheless, its seeds are clearly discernible in the gropings of the seventeenth century in which the concept emerged of a commercial economy with its own momentum and logic, capable of sustained economic progress mutually beneficial to the groups and nations involved in it.

I believe, in sum, that the following broad reconstruction is consistent with Polanyi's argument. The sixteenth century witnessed a dramatic growth in the scope and strength of market forces. This engendered in the next century a profound crisis in the meaning and guiding principles of everyday British life. From this crisis emerged the market mentality which reached its mature intellectual expression in classical economics and its institutional, practical fruition in the nineteenth century. Appleby's valuable book demonstrates the origin of the idea of the disembedded economy, classicism developed the ideology of such an economy and led to a dramatic social experiment, and Polanyi among others interpreted the results and implications of this experiment.

THE DISEMBEDDED ECONOMY AND THE MARKET MYTH

Polanyi drew from economic anthropology and history the lesson that the general condition of the human economy and society was that of the economy being embedded in society.

> The outstanding discovery of recent historical and anthropological research is that man's economy, as a rule, is submerged in his social relationships. He does not act so as to safeguard his individual interest in the possession of material goods; he acts so as to safeguard his social standing, his social claims, his social assets. He values material goods only insofar as they serve this end. Neither the process of production nor that of distribution is linked to specific economic interests attached to the possession of goods; but every single step in that process is geared to a number of social interests which eventually ensure that the required step be taken. These interests will be very different in a small hunting or fishing community from those in a vast despotic society, but in either case the economic [substantive] system will be run on noneconomic [noncalculative] motives. (*GT*, p. 46)

I wish to be as clear as possible here. One objection might be that in the modern social economy, people still pursue economic activity in order to sustain their way of life or social situs. The economy is always instituted by a socialization process which moulds individual character toward the ethical, aesthetical, and instrumental norms, standards, and practices which are needed to participate in the economy. This much is true of all social economies in that all must integrate economic activity by means of systems of communication and sanction. These systems inform individuals as to the behaviour expected of them and of others, and of the rewards and penalties that they can apply to others or expect to be applied to themselves in cases where expected behaviour is or is not forthcoming. Yet the modern economy is different because its rules and norms are shaped by the requirements of the economy. The predominant line of causation is reversed. The economy was previously subordinate to the other social realms which constrained economic activity and set the hue and temper of social life. The modern economy is, by contrast, superordinate to social life in general. Economic desiderata influence family life, friendships, leisure, and mythology, actively so, in a way totally different from the more passively limiting influence of the economy in previous eras.

Of particular importance is the subordinate position of the motive of self-gain in earlier societies (see *PAME*, p. 66, and *GT*, p. 47). This motive is the hallmark of the modern disembedded economy. Calculated self-gain is the economic logic sui generis. In contrast, the embedded economy has no inherent logic of its own; there is no distinctive behaviour which can be labelled economic in terms of its motivation and guiding principles. There is, of course, an objective substantive function, nature's decreed technological interaction of humanity with the rest of nature. But the subjective meaning of substantive economic activity is not implicit in that objective function. Moreover, in the terminology of functionalism, the provisioning function may be latent, inexplicit. Instead, the economic necessity of provisioning a livelihood is carried out in the context of social life in general.

> As long as [the redistribution and reciprocity] forms of integration prevail, no concept of an economy need arise. The elements of the economy are here embedded in non-economic institutions, the economic process itself being instituted through kinship, marriage, age-groups, secret societies, totemic associations, and public

> solemnities. The term "economic life" would have no obvious meaning. (*PAME*, p. 84)

In other words, the economy was anonymous in premodern societies. Polanyi developed the concept of the disembedded economy in order to uncover the reversal of this anonymity in recent history (*PAME*, p. 81), and to get rid of the modern 'ingrained notion that the economy is a field of experience of which human beings have necessarily always been conscious' (*PAME*, p. 119). In earlier societies, the problem of livelihood was given less conscious attention and there was generally no term for the economy, even in the substantive sense (*PAME*, p. 85). The contrast could not be sharper between this and the fetishistic preoccupation with matters economic in modern society. Modern calculativeness is combined with individual gainmanship and this combination of the intellect and the ego is a protean, combustible institutional compound, the source of the success and failure of the modern era.

None of this is to say that premodern society consisted of people who were intrinsically more altruistic, less selfish than modern man. 'The human passions, good or bad, [were] merely directed towards noneconomic ends' (*GT*, p. 47). Selfishness and the motive of self-gain were undoubtedly present – after all, there is literary and institutional evidence that they were condemned and lamented, and this is proof enough of their existence. And, this is the point at hand: the gain motive was constrained and held in check by its interwovenness with religious, familial, and political motivations. Self-gain was but one thread in the social fabric such that no whole cloth could ever be made from it. The economic motive is rarely paramount to the individual in premodern society because his livelihood is guaranteed by virtue of his belonging to the community, unless, of course, that community were to face an aggregate interruption in its means of livelihood. The social motives of maintaining one's status by fulfilling one's obligations (such as regard for others) and observing social taboos (such as avoiding an unseemly concern for material gain), however, is clearly of crucial concern to the individual. His social ties guarantee his livelihood and it is those social ties which are subjectively meaningful for him (*GT*, p. 46). From the social point of view, reciprocal concern for others is important because it secures cooperation in the substantive function which is vitally necessary to social reproduction. This is in sharp contrast to the modern economy in which gain is promoted to a pillar institution. The peculiarity of the social economy which came to maturity in the nineteenth century

> was precisely that it rested on economic foundations. Other societies and other civilizations, too, were limited by the material conditions of their existence. . . . All types of societies are limited by economic factors. Nineteenth century civilization alone was economic in a different and distinctive sense, for it chose to base itself on a motive only rarely acknowledged as valid in the history of human societies, and certainly never before raised to the level of a justification of action and behavior in everyday life, namely, gain. The self-regulating market system was uniquely derived from this principle. (*GT*, p. 30)

At the aggregate level, the institutionalization of gain is manifested by economic growth, i.e. the pay-off at the social level for the new economic organization was the steady improvement in aggregate output.

> Mankind was in the grip, not of new motives, but of new mechanisms. Briefly, the strain sprang from the zone of the market; from there it spread . . ., [eventually] comprising the whole of society. . . . [A] civilization was being disrupted by the blind action of soulless institutions the only purpose of which was the automatic increase of material welfare. (*GT*, p. 219)

The motive of gain and the institutional complex of the supply–demand–price system came to be viewed as comprising an autonomous sphere of human activity, 'the economic system, governed by economic motives, and subject to the economic principle of formal rationality (i.e. economizing)' (*PAME*, p. 132). The 'sociological situations which make individuals partake in economic life' were created by 'specifically economic institutions'. These institutions 'are activated by economic motives and governed by laws that are specifically economic'. The economy is conceived to be 'working without the conscious intervention of human authority' (*PAME*, p. 82). This is the disembedded economy: an autonomous sphere of human activity, self-motivating by greed or the threat of hunger and self-governing through a system of price-making markets. Adam Smith seized order from apparent chaos by insisting that an invisible hand was at work. His followers, especially James Mill and

Ricardo, refined his themes on the self-regulating economy and further isolated the economic motive from the other mainsprings of human action. Indeed, it is probable that Mill and Ricardo, with their pathological antimony toward government, implanted a much more stringent *laissez-faire* attitude into the self-regulating market conception than ever crossed Smith's mind.[11]

Historically, then, the economy is first stripped of the anonymity in which it was located in early society. This began in Archaic Greece and was completed in the mercantilist era. Consciousness of the economy was first met by political administration. In the liberal era, this response was done away with and the aggregate purpose of provisioning was again obscured. The consciousness of the economy was shifted to the micro level, and infused with the motive of self-gain. The aggregate provisioning function was to be secured automatically through the moulding of this micro consciousness by a competitive milieu. From the social point of view, this conception embodies the achievement of purpose, i.e. provisioning, without purposive activity toward that end. For Polanyi, this conception is utopian, mythical. He refers often to the utopian experiment carried out under the banner of the market myth. In his view, the experiment was a disastrous failure imperiling the social order itself. The market myth neglects the primacy of society and leaves social life open to disruption by the disturbances of an uncontrolled market process. Provisioning is an integral part of social reproduction, providing the material wherewithal for the continuation of society as a going concern. The self-regulating market's lack of dependability threatens social reproduction. The market myth also generates character traits which are inconsistent with social stability. Social cohesion is undermined by the excessive and inadequately controlled gain orientation. This is well expressed by the craftsman to whom Charles Dickens' Ebeneezer Scrooge was apprenticed. When queried about some aspect of business with the implication that he was missing profit, he replied that business could not be run for mere gain but had to be run so as to preserve a way of life. The self-regulating market economy undermines traditions and this vital function of preservation.

The disembedded economy does not mean that economy is in fact autonomous since, as already noted above, society, culture, and polity have to support economic behaviour in many ways. For example, children must be raised to respond to relative prices, balance chequebooks, drive cars, and strive for success;

and contracts must be enforced and standards regulated by government. The distinction between the embedded and disembedded is, moreover, a matter of degree (*PAME*, p. 82). The distinction is nonetheless vital to understanding modern society because the market myth and the glorification of gain produce a perverse tendency for economic considerations to dominate social, cultural, and political life. These other aspects become mere adjuncts of the economy. 'Society [becomes] imbedded in the economic system, rather than vice versa' (*PAME*, p. 131 or *GT*, p. 57). The result is the economic control of social activity. To elaborate the peril to society posed by the tendency for economic motivation and expectations to dominate social and political life, and the social reaction to this peril, I now turn to Polanyi's concepts of the fictitious commodities and the protective response.

THE FICTITIOUS COMMODITIES AND THE PROTECTIVE RESPONSE

The 'economistic transformation' is, then, the intentional creation of a competitive market economy, the regulation of which is to be left to its own internal devices. This transformation was effected in obedience to the dictates of the economistic fallacy. These actions, this mentality, blind to the delicate interaction between economy and society, disembedded the economy and literally imperiled society itself. The gauge of the embeddedness or disembeddedness of an economy is the place occupied by land and labour. As I have already noted, the industrialized market economy requires a relatively secure demand for industrial output and supply of natural and human resources. These requirements were met simultaneously as the traditional social ties linking man to nature were dissolved and replaced with new linkages, the commodity production, cash nexus. To gain access to the raw materials and instruments of production, including their subsistence, the labouring population must sell their labour in the market. Free or wage labourers are free to strike wage bargains with the employer of their choice, but they are not free to avoid doing so because they must earn wages to survive. Raw materials, land or natural resources, are also commoditized. Human productive activity is then linked to its objective basis, the rest of nature, by the market process. Money must also be commoditized because its expression of relative prices is the medium of the communication and sanction system of the market economy, i.e. money is the language of organizing production and distribution on a commodity production basis. The crucial step, then, is the treating of land and labour as commodities (*LM*, p. 10); money is also so treated.

The designation *commodity* is important. Polanyi defined commodities 'as objects produced for sale on the market' (*GT*, p. 72). Articles produced for direct use or ceremonial gift-giving are not commodities. Even output sold on the market does not constitute commodity production so long as the objects sold are only the incidental surplus of production for direct use. Commodity production is the specialized production of objects for sale on the market. This specialization makes production dependent on the market: marketability is the sine qua non of production. This is the same distinction that Marx made and Polanyi, like Marx, was concerned about the implications of a social organization which instituted the essential function of provisioning on the basis of producing articles for sale in a system of price-making markets. Polanyi underscored the utopian character of such an organization with the concept of fictitious commodities.

> But labor, land, and money are obviously *not* commodities; the postulate that anything that is bought and sold must have been produced for sale is emphatically untrue in regard to them. In other words, according to the empirical definition of a commodity they are not commodities. Labor is only another name for a human activity which goes with life itself, which in its turn is not produced for sale but for entirely different reasons, nor can that activity be detached from the rest of life, be stored or mobilized; land is only another name for nature, which is not produced by man; actual money, finally, is merely a token of purchasing power which, as a rule, is not produced at all, but comes into being through the mechanism of banking or state finance. None of them is produced for sale. The commodity description of labor, land, and money is entirely fictitious. (*GT*, p. 72)

Polanyi was not denying that land, labour, and money were in fact exchanged like commodities. Organized markets for exchanging them certainly existed, and, indeed, had to exist in order for a market economy to exist. The commodity fictions supply 'a vital organizing principle' (*GT*, p. 73) for such an economy, the operation of which

> means that there must be markets for every element of industry; that in these markets each of these elements is organized into a supply and a demand group; and that each element has a price which interacts with supply and demand. These markets . . . are interconnected and form One Big Market.
>
> The crucial point is this: land, labor, and money are essential elements of industry; they also must be organized in markets; in fact, these markets form an absolutely vital part of the [market] economic system. (*GT*, p. 72)

In Hawtrey's words, the Big Market functions by making 'the relative market value of all commodities mutually consistent' (*GT*, p. 72n).

The market economy, then, must treat these industrial elements *as if* they were commodities. Polanyi's point is no mere semantic trifle. It was central to his argument that the commodity fictions had to exist for a market economy to exist. The fictional, or mystified, bases of the market economy indicated the mythical character of the self-regulating market economy. An image of the economy founded on fictional premises is not a realistic conception of social organization; it is a thoroughly utopian conception. Polanyi went on to examine the implications of this utopian attempt at reconstruction of the social economy. That is, he asked: What is the result of a social organization which treats land, labour, and money as if they were commodities?

The institutionalization of the labour market required reversing the historically ubiquitous relationships between man, society, and subsistence. All earlier societies, short of social famine, guaranteed the individual a livelihood by virtue of his membership in the group or society. The labour market, in contrast, requires the threat of hunger, as is seen in Ricardian theory where 'only the penalty of starvation . . . was deemed capable of creating a functioning labour market' (*GT*, p. 164). The necessary social thought and practice which constitute a labour market developed through several stages, 'the final stage was reached with the application of "nature's penalty", hunger' (*GT*, p. 165). In England, this final stage is symbolized by the Poor Law Reform Act of 1834 which stigmatized living on the public dole and established the principle of less eligibility, i.e. the dole should be well below the going minimum wage rate.

The implications of the commoditization of labour are far reaching. The wage is set by market forces, there is no social entity with the responsibility to assure that the wage is sufficient for a minimally decent livelihood. Such a minimum wage policy is antithetical to the market economy, witness the conservative argument today that minimum wage legislation causes unemployment. After all, if labour will work at the offered wage, which must decline with a surplus supply of labour, there can be no unemployment. Of course, this also requires that labour be prepared to relocate geographically and occupationally, as Ludwig von Mises observed: if workers 'reduced their demands and changed their locations and occupations according to the requirements of the labour market, they could eventually find work' (*GT*, p. 176). This is a prescription for social instability. If workers must move their families when the market dictates, how can roots be put down and a way of life which is structured and meaningful be sustained? How can professional standards and tradition be maintained under such occupational flux? As Polanyi observed, Mises' remark

> sums up the position [of labor] under a system based on the postulate of the commodity character of labor. It is not for the commodity to decide where it should be offered for sale, to what purpose it should be used, at what price it should be allowed to change hands, and in what manner it should be consumed or destroyed. (*GT*, p. 176)

The wider functions of the work process beyond mere production of output and earning an income are obscured. Work reveals to the individual much about the character of his society and his role in it. Work as the meaningful relation to the natural environment, work as the cement binding a way of life, work as the source of an individual's social and self-image, all of these and more are cast aside by the commodity fiction of labour.

The case is similar for land, i.e. the natural environment. The institutionalization of the natural resources market occurred in several stages, principally the commercialization of the soil, increasing output to feed a growing urban population, and extension of the European organization all around the globe (*GT*, p. 179). In the English case, the symbolic step was the repeal of the Corn Laws in 1846. These laws, as Malthus among others contended, were necessary to protect the agrarian way of life from destruction, and this way of life had important traditional functions. Agri*culture* is a way of life far different from agribusiness.

> The economic function is but one of many vital functions of land. It invests man's life with stability; it is the site of his habitation; it is a condition of his physical safety; it is the landscape and the seasons. We might as well imagine his being born without hands and feet as carrying on his life without land. And yet to separate land from man and organize society in such a way as to satisfy the requirements of a real-estate market was a vital part of the utopian concept of a market economy. (*GT*, p. 178)

The commercialization of land, then and now, gives the control of land to mere owners who can evict or exact recompense from those who have used or would use the land. In the American 1930s, families whose lineages for a century or more were born and buried on the land were cast off by the financial interests. The same process has long been at work along the interface between traditional and market economies.

The case of the commodity fiction with respect to money is less obvious but no less valid.

> Even capitalist business itself had to be sheltered from the unrestricted working of the market mechanism. . . .
>
> [I]n the case of productive enterprise as in that of man and nature the peril was real and objective. The need for protection arose on account of the manner in which the supply of money was organized under a market system. Modern central banking, in effect, was essentially a device developed for the purpose of offering protection without which the market would have destroyed its own children, the business enterprises of all kinds. (*GT*, p. 192)

The classical conception of the quantity theory of money holds that a reduction in the money supply of one-half would lead only to a like reduction in nominal prices, leaving the all-important relative prices, and thus also business, undisturbed. That is true so far as it goes, but in the process business might be destroyed. Comparative statics analysis neglects the time path and pace of adjustment. Lags in adjustment are merely the untidy affairs of reality. The same neglect of reality is evident in the comparative statics argument that unemployment must eventually be swept away by falling wages. How long the adjustment takes, and the impacts it delivers, are critical to realistic policy but invisible to comparative statics equilibrium analysis. Money is the language of industrial organization, and commoditized money in a self-regulating market 'is incompatible with industrial production' (*GT*, p. 193).

To return to the general question, what are the social implications of an economy operated upon the commodity fictions?, Polanyi's answer is clear:

> To allow the market mechanism to be the sole director of the fate of human beings and their natural environment, indeed, even of the amount and use of purchasing power, would result in the demolition of society. . . . Undoubtedly, labor, land, and money markets *are* essential to a market economy. But no society could stand the effects of such a system of crude fictions . . . unless its human and natural substance as well as its business organization was protected against the ravages of this satanic mill.
>
> The extreme artificiality of market economy is rooted in the fact that the process of production itself is here organized in the form of buying and selling. (*GT*, p. 73)

The commoditization of land, labour, and money, if unchecked, would destroy society. The impossibility of a self-regulating market economy is shown in the inconsistency of such an arrangement with the continuation of a functioning social order. To subject the substantive provisioning of society to an unfettered market mechanism would destroy social organization.

And yet it is clear that the nineteenth century witnessed an attempt to establish such a market economy. What was the result of this effort? In answering this question, Polanyi's analysis demonstrates its considerable strength. Polanyi argued that the effort to establish a self-regulating market economy was necessarily accompanied by a contrary effort to protect society from the disruption which otherwise would have occurred. The market imperative toward extending commoditization generated a protective imperative to safeguard social organization from the effects of commoditization. 'Human society would have been annihilated but for protective countermoves which blunted the action of this self-destructive mechanism' (*GT*,

p. 76). The protective countermoves are many and diverse. Governments intervened to protect labour with legislation regulating child and women labour, working conditions, workday lengths, and subsequent income maintenance programmes. Legislation was enacted on land use planning, resource conservation, pollution control, and modern comprehensive environmental protection. The case for other fictitious commodity, money or purchasing power, is less obvious but no less strong for it. Polanyi's reference was to money as the medium by which the division of labour is integrated. To allow the money markets free play would subject the organization of provisioning to catastrophic instability. The governmental response has been central banking, capital market regulations, and aggregate demand management.

> Therefore, in respect to business a very similar situation existed as in respect to the natural and human substance of society. The self-regulating market was a threat to them all, and for essentially similar reasons. And if factory legislation and social laws were required to protect industrial man from the implications of the commodity fiction in regard to labor power, if land laws and agrarian tariffs were called into being by the necessity of protecting natural resources and the culture of the countryside against the implications of the commodity fiction in respect to them, it was equally true that central banking and the management of the monetary system were needed to keep manufactures and other productive enterprises safe from the harm involved in the commodity fiction as applied to money. Paradoxically enough, not human beings and natural resources only but also the organization of capitalistic production itself had to be sheltered from the devastating effects of a self-regulating market. (*GT*, p. 132)

It is important to note two additional points. First, it is not valid to present the protective state interventions as resulting from a leftward ideological shift or the increasing political power of labour. There is no universal ideological stance or political statism which can encompass the breadth of intervention involved. Very often the programmes were enacted by those quite enamoured with a pro-market ideology. The comprehensive feature is not ideology or political interest group, but the necessity of countering the disruptions of the market process. This is important for, as a moment's reflection will point up, Polanyi's case is directly counter to the view of economic liberalism. Polanyi argues, as I have reviewed above, that the installation of the self-regulating market economy was a matter of conscious design, not spontaneous historical forces. For the liberal, also discussed above, the market is ubiquitous and the market economy inevitably emerges because it is 'natural'. On the other hand, Polanyi argues that the trend away from the self-regulating market is spontaneous; the liberal sees this trend to be the result of a collectivist intellectual drift or of protectionist economic interests shortsightedly using the power of the state in their own interests.

Polanyi goes to great lengths to counter the 'myth of the antiliberal conspiracy', i.e. that economic liberalism has not been fairly tried because its principles have not been completely followed. He notes that the 'eminent liberal, Dicey' undertook an inquiry into the anti-liberal, collectivist trend only to find evidence contrary to his purposes. According to Polanyi, Dicey found 'that no evidence of the existence of such a trend could be traced *save the acts of legislation themselves*', that there was no evidence 'of any deliberate intention to extend the functions of the state', and that instead the legislation appeared to be 'spontaneous, undirected by opinion, and actuated by a purely pragmatic spirit' (*GT*, p. 141). Polanyi cites several other factors which militate against the anti-liberal conspiracy: 'the amazing diversity of the matters on which action was taken', the decidedly pro-liberal views of sponsors of legislation, the evolution of specific problem areas to intervention, and the wide variety of countries involved (*GT*, pp. 145–8).

> Thus under the most varied slogans, with very different motivations a multitude of parties and social strata put into effect almost exactly the same measures in a series of countries in respect to a large number of complicated subjects. There is . . . nothing more absurd than to infer that they were secretly actuated by the same ideological preconceptions or narrow group interests as the legend of the antiliberal conspiracy would have it. On the contrary, everything tends to support the assumption that objective reasons of a stringent nature forced the hands of the legislators. (*GT*, pp. 147–8.)

The protective response 'possessed all the unmistakable characteristics of a spontaneous reaction' (*GT*, p. 149).

The second additional point reinforces the first. The protective response is by no means limited to action through the state apparata. The attempted default of the state of the vital area of protecting the social basis of the lives of its members, left this protective function to organizational measures of the populace, in and out of government.[12] Imperialism and nationalism are banners of protective ideology, their practice is the political, diplomatic, and military administration of economy. Combinations, trusts, and cartels are protectively motivated and operated. Even the modern corporation, the central economic institution of modern capitalism, can be viewed as part of the protective response. The principal animus behind the corporate revolution is the urge to stabilize and control the exigencies of the corporate environment, and these exigencies are largely the uncertainties concomitant to the operation of the market mechanism. I am convinced that economic and business historians will eventually view the modern corporation in this light, and that corporate officials will do likewise, notwithstanding the free enterprise ideology which remains strong to this time. After all, the image of the corporation as an institution intent upon ensuring the orderly operation of the vital provisioning function is not only more correct but also far more salutary than the traditional typification of the corporation as a profit-mongering monopolist.

THE DOUBLE MOVEMENT AND INTERVENTIONIST DRIFT

Much is learned about the nature of the corporate–welfare state when it is viewed as the culmination of what Polanyi referred to as the *double movement* of the nineteenth century. The blending of the two institutional motivators, the self-regulating market and the protective response, underscores the spontaneous character of the latter. The one universal factor behind this response is the necessity of protecting society against the disruption inherent in the automatic market economy. The double movement also uncovers the principal institutional dynamic of the twentieth-century democratic industrial social economy. In Polanyi's words:

> Social history in the nineteenth century was thus the result of a double movement. . . . While on the one hand markets spread all over the face of the globe and the amount of goods involved grew to unbelievable proportions, on the other hand a network of measures and policies was integrated into powerful institutions

> designed to check the action of the market relative to labor, land, and money. . . . Society protected itself against the perils inherent in a self-regulating market system – this was the one comprehensive feature in the history of the age. (*GT*, p. 76)

The double movement expresses the two 'organizing principles' at work in democratic industrial society, the 'principle of economic liberalism, aiming at the establishment of a self-regulating market', and, 'the principle of social protection aiming at the conservation of man and nature as well as productive organization' (*GT*, p. 132). These two principles each had concomitant class or sectional interests which, generally speaking, represented them in socio-political life. The middle class, the business interests, generally promoted the principle of economic liberalism, though as I have shown above, the business interests too had a stake and role in the protective response. Moreover, the other classes or strata, workers, peasants, and gentry, were not altogether devoid of interests coincident to the principle of economic liberalism because they too benefited from the growth in production and employment spawned by the protean, if utopian, social organization of market capitalism. Still, business protection was largely limited to the protection of productive organization against the instability of the utopian experiment. The business classes

> had no organ to sense the dangers involved in the exploitation of the physical strength of the worker, the destruction of family life, the devastation of neighborhoods, the denudation of forests, the pollution of rivers, the deterioration of craft standards, the disruption of folkways, and the general degradation of existence including housing and arts, as well as the innumerable forms of private and public life which do not affect profits. (*GT*, p. 133)

The middle class protected prices and profits but 'this disqualified them as the keepers of other interests as vital to a good life as the furtherance of production' (*GT*, p. 133). This further protection was made by the working, peasant, and landed classes, whose interests were more sensitive in this regard because they were closely bound up with the perils of commodity production of land and labour. Again, though, Polanyi warned against absolutizing these class interests: 'at one time or another, each social class stood, even if unconsciously, for interests wider than its own' (*GT*, p. 133). Polanyi also distinguished his theory from the 'crude class theory of social development' expounded by *popular* Marxism (*GT*, p. 151). Such a view would play into the hands of the anti-liberal conspiracy thesis as well as fatally oversimplify the 'breadth and comprehensiveness of the protectionist movement' (*GT*, p. 154).

This conception of market capitalist society indicates two important aspects of its institutional change: entrepreneurial dynamism and interventionist drift. Entrepreneurial decisions over the structure and location of output and technology have had extreme external impacts. Decisions such as those which have rendered obsolete fixed capital or labour skills, eradicated product lines or industries, or altered the development path of communities or regions have been made upon the basis of entrepreneurial calculation. The dynamism of capitalism is not difficult to account for if the distributive impacts of change are assayed. It is an instructive oversimplification to view the entrepreneurs as the principal beneficiaries of their decisions, but with society absorbing a substantial portion of the costs. Society's interest beyond prices and profits had to be protected by the actions of workers, peasants, and *rentier*. The protective actions against entrepreneurial dynamism constitute interventionist drift, given the prevalence of the market myth which made it impossible to grasp the true character and meaning of interventionism. These actions are a necessary response to the utopian experiment of market capitalism; as I have shown, this is the sole universal at work in the protective response. The market myth, by concealing the utopian character of the nineteenth-century institutional experimentation, also conceals the true character of the protective response. The market myth blinds man in a thousand ways to the role of the state in economy, especially the sadly neglected role of regulating the pace of social change (*GT*, p. 37). In general, the 'eclipse of political thinking was the intellectual deficiency' of the market myth (*LM*, p. 15).

The disembedded economy creates the semblance of an economy as an autonomous system governed by its own laws. The application of noneconomic criteria to the market economy is then of necessity viewed as an intervention in an otherwise self-functioning sphere of human activity. Nowhere is this more clear than in the modern liberal economist's insistence that justification of state intervention must be made by citing some failing of the market mechanism. No matter that the modern liberal justifies in this fashion a wide range of state intervention, the persistence of the market myth in economic thinking is patently clear. The persistence of the basic competitive market, maximizing model in economic thinking up to the present time is *de rigueur* among historians of economic thought, despite the considerable changes associated with the marginal and Keynesian revolutions.[13] It is symptomatic of the persistence of this intellectual deficiency that state intervention is frequently made to shore up the market and achieve the competitive solution which would be forthcoming if only the extraordinary and socially disastrous assumptions of the self-regulating market conception should be sustained in reality.

Intervention in the actual market process in the name of the self-regulating market ideal is a fatally deficient intellectual purview. It engenders the comforting semblance that the market economy is essentially sound but requires occasional and abnormal supplementation through other social mechanisms. This is the myth of interventionist drift: the belief that only piecemeal and reactive intervention is necessary to maintaining the operation of the otherwise autonomous market economy. A correct understanding of the protective response exposes the fallacy of this myth as surely as that of the market myth. The protective response is, inherently, not a supplement to the market economy but a signal to replace that child of utopian experimentation. The self-protective response of society is 'incompatible with the functioning' of the market economy (*GT*, p. 129); its function *vis-à-vis* the markets for the fictitious commodities is 'to prevent their establishment or to interfere with their free functioning, once established' (*GT*, p. 201).

> The natural aim of all social protection was to destroy such an institution and make its existence impossible. Actually, the labor market was allowed to retain its main function only on condition that wages and conditions of work, standards and regulations should be such as would safeguard the human character of the alleged commodity, labor. To argue that social legislation, factory laws, unemployment insurance, and, above all, trade unions have not interfered with the mobility of labor and the flexibility of wages, as is sometimes done, is to imply that those institutions have entirely failed in their purpose, which was exactly that of interfering with the laws of supply and demand in respect to human labor, and removing it from the orbit of the market. (*GT*, p. 177)

The cases of land and money are the same as that of labour.

The inconsistency of protective response with the market economy is easily seen in the effects of protectionism on the fabled automaticity of the market mechanism.

> Protectionism helped to transform competitive markets into monopolistic ones. Less and less could markets be described as autonomous and automatic mechanisms of competing atoms. More and more were individuals replaced by associations, men and capital united to noncompeting groups. Economic adjustment became slow and difficult. The self-regulation of markets was gravely hampered. Eventually, unadjusted price and cost structures prolonged depressions, unadjusted equipment retarded the liquidation of unprofitable investments, unadjusted price and income levels caused social tension. And whatever the market in question – labor, land, or money – the strain would transcend the economic zone and the balance would have to be restored by political means. Nevertheless, the institutional separation of the political from the economic sphere was constitutive to market society and had to be maintained whatever the tension involved. This was the other source of disruptive strain. (*GT*, p. 218)

Whatever automaticity the market economy possessed, it constituted a threat to society and was impaired in the response to that threat. Each impairment creates anew the need for further intervention. Had the libertarian charge of creeping socialism been instead creeping interventionism, free of the myth of the anti-liberal conspiracy, it would have been largely correct. But a socialist drift is a thing apart from an interventionist drift, and it is in the latter that modern man has attempted to restore the primacy of society against its subordination to the requirements of the utopian experiment with a self-regulating market economy.

> To sum up. The countermove against economic liberalism and *laissez-faire* possessed all the unmistakable characteristics of a spontaneous reaction. At innumerable disconnected points it set in without any traceable links between the interests directly affected or any ideological conformity between them. . . . Also it could be shown that a closely similar change from *laissez-faire* to "collectivism" took place in various countries at a definite stage of their industrial development, pointing to the depth and

independence of the underlying causes of the process so superficially credited by economic liberals to changing moods or sundry interests. Finally, analysis reveals that not even radical adherents of economic liberalism could escape the rule which makes *laissez-faire* inapplicable to advanced industrial conditions; for in the critical case of trade union law and antitrust regulations extreme liberals themselves had to call for manifold interventions of the state. . . . Even free trade and competition required intervention to be workable. The liberal myth of the "collectivist" conspiracy of the 1870's and 1880's is contrary to all the facts.

Our own interpretation of the double movement is, we find, borne out by the evidence. For if market economy was a threat to the human and natural components of the social fabric, as we insisted, what else would one expect than an urge on the part of a great variety of people to press for some sort of protection? . . . Also, one would expect this to happen without any theoretical or intellectual preconceptions on their part, and irrespective of their attitudes towards the principles underlying a market economy. . . . Moreover, we suggested that comparative history of governments might offer quasi-experimental support of our thesis if particular interests could be shown to be independent of the specific ideologies present in a number of different countries. . . . Finally, the behavior of liberals themselves proved that the maintenance of freedom of trade – in our terms, of a self-regulating market – far from excluding intervention, in effect, demanded such action, and that liberals themselves regularly called for compulsory action on the part of the state as in the case of trade union law and antitrust laws. Thus nothing could be more decisive than the evidence of history as to which of the two contending interpretations of the double movement was correct: that of the economic liberal who maintained that his policy never had a chance, but was strangled by shortsighted trade unionists, Marxist intellectuals, greedy manufacturers, and reactionary landlords; or that of his critics, who can point to the universal "collectivist" reaction against the expansion of market economy in the second half of the nineteenth century as conclusive proof of the peril to society inherent in the utopian principle of a self-regulating market. (*GT*, p. 149–50)

5 Industrialism and Freedom

Having traced the evolution of market capitalism, its congenital defects, the protective response they spawned, and the drift thusly generated toward the corporate–welfare state, and in light of the rife institutional crisis which permeates that social order, it is necessary to pause and take stock. I have argued that the corporate–welfare state manifests a spontaneous social movement unconsciously bent on returning the economy to its traditional or historical place in society, namely, an economy politically administered or otherwise socially embedded. Several questions emerge. What are the implications of the analysis with respect to industrialism, the patent historical sibling of market capitalism? How does the present analysis compare with the logic of industrial reform and social change which has been a key theme of American Institutionalism from its precursors, through its founders, to its current champions? Together, considerations of these two questions will enable me to suggest the strength of Polanyi's interpretation of social change in industrial market capitalism, and lead me to a final and most important question: What is the place of freedom in the emerging order? Is freedom in fact so integrally intertwined with the market economy that it is institutionally inconsistent with the administered economy?

INDUSTRIALISM VERSUS MARKET CAPITALISM

The Industrial Revolution and the rise of market capitalism are not only historically contemporaneous but interdependent in myriad and complicated ways. Nonetheless, they must be distinguished because the lasting importance of each to the livelihood of man is radically different. 'The nineteenth century gave birth to two sets of events of a very different order of magnitude: the machine age, a development of millennial range; and the market system, an initial adjustment to that development' (*LM*, p. xlviii). The machine age, or better, *industrialism*, ushered in by the Industrial Revolution, is a radical and permanent change in the way mankind makes its living. It is centred in the technological locus which is the core of the substantive economy, and it is a change of epochal magnitude. Industrialism is the third great epoch of human history since the Old Stone Age, following the Neolithic and plough agricultural epochs.

Market capitalism, on the other hand, is merely the 'initial response to the challenge of the Industrial Revolution' (*PAME*, p. 59). Not surprisingly, it was Polanyi's considered judgment that it was the wrong response, or at least one that is long since obsolete. The social disaster of the nineteenth century, a disaster which continues to be inherited by every generation, was not, and is not, a product of industrialism per se but of industrialism as instituted through means of market capitalism. '*The congenital weakness of nineteenth century society was not that it was industrial but that it was a market society*' (*GT*, p. 250). The changes brought about in production by the Industrial Revolution were superimposed on, or planted in the bed of, a commercial society. Large-scale, capital-intensive production is not practical without a reasonably secure supply of labour and materials and availability of customers, i.e. purchasing power. But in a society in which political thinking had been eclipsed, and therefore no administrative solutions to this problem of security obtained, there was only one answer and that answer was *the market*.

> [T]he more complicated industrial production became, the more numerous were the elements of industry the supply of which had to be safeguarded. Three of these, of course, were of outstanding importance: labor, land, and money. In a commercial society their supply could be organized in one way only: by being made available for purchase. Hence, they would have to be organized for sale on the market – in other words, as commodities. The extension of the market mechanism to the elements of industry – labor, land and money – was the inevitable consequence of the introduction of the factory system in a commercial society. The elements of industry had to be on sale. (*GT*, p. 75)

It was, then, 'machine production in a commercial society' that necessitated the birth of the fictitious commodities, the effects of which were discussed above in Chapter 4. The buying and selling of actual commodities, artifacts, poses no threat to the fabric of society, but similar treatment of the fictitious commodities is a different matter: 'the dislocation caused by such devices must disjoint man's relationships and threaten his natural habitat with annihilation' (*GT*, p. 42).

The point should be stressed: it is not to machine industrial technology but to its situs in market capitalism that one must look for the cause of so many of the perils that face a humane way of life in industrial civilization. Take, for example, the destruction of a sense of community and the concomitant rootless, structureless psyches of individuals. In his very popular book, *Small is Beautiful*, E. F. Schumacher places a great deal of stress on the footloose, structureless pattern of modern life. He blames this condition on the technology which permits physical mobility. 'A highly developed transport and communications system has one immensely powerful effect: it makes people *footloose*.'[1] Schumacher, however, offers no explanation of why the technology per se destroys community structure, except to say that prior to the advent of that technology, 'the structure was simply there, because people were relatively immobile'.[2] But surely the technology is permissive only, it does not explain the profound and essentially *sociological* phenomena in question. The real cause, as Schumacher suggests at other places, lies in the market economy and society which determine the selection and deployment of the technology. In the market society, the natural and social reality behind the exchange process is neglected; 'the market is the institutionalization of individualism and non-responsibility'.[3] The market economy is fuelled by this neglect and the individual psyches that result. 'The modern economy is propelled by a frenzy of greed and indulges in an orgy of envy, and these are not accidental features but the very causes of its expansionist success.'[4] This is very similar to Polanyi's insistence that the defect of the market economy is not the mere existence of selfishness and the motive of gain, but rather the elevation of this motive to a central and predominant place in the social order.

Irresponsibility is destructive of community because the latter has much to do with reciprocal obligation, responsiveness to each other's needs, and commitment to give-and-take. This antipathy between the market economy and community is evident in the externalities which are so prevalent in the market economy. In a community setting, people are aware of their impacts on each other, responsive to each other, and externalities are minimized. This is further evidenced by the exalted mobility of labour, a factor Schumacher links to footlooseness. The importance of the mobility factor and its inconsistency with community roots was made clear by Frank Knight in his classic typification of the market economy. Among the assumptions he cited for perfect competition were that there be 'no exercise of constraint over any individual by another individual or "society"; each controls his own activities with a view to results which accrue to him individually'. There must also be 'complete absence of physical obstacles to the making, execution, and changing of plans at will; that is, there must be "perfect mobility"'.[5] Even more clearly to the point, Knight continues:

> Every member of the society is to act as an individual only, in entire independence of all other persons. To complete his independence he must be free from social wants, prejudices, preferences, or repulsions, or any values which are not completely manifested in market dealing. Exchange of finished goods is the only form of relation between individuals, or at least there is no other form which influences economic conduct. And in exchanges between individuals, no interest of persons not parties to the exchange are to be concerned, either for good or ill.[6]

In a footnote, Knight qualifies this formulation to allow for families – somewhat: 'dependent members of the society must be *completely* dependent on some particular individual in it. The wants of any dependent person will then operate only through wants on his behalf felt by his sponsor. . . . We simply regard the independent members of the society as having normal solicitudes in regard to families, etc. . . .'. I say somewhat because this description could only apply to a narrow, nuclear family and not to an extended family of any significant degree. It certainly would not befit a situation of extensive community relationships.

Of course, Knight was making an idealized typology, using '"heroic" abstraction' with regard to an 'imaginary society'. Nonetheless, he did contend that the 'assumptions . . . are idealizations or purifications of tendencies which hold good more or less in reality'.[7] Undeniably, the mobility of labour is very important to the functioning of an actual market economy. Von Mises did not have an ideal construct in mind when he remarked that if workers 'did not act as trade unionists, but reduced their demands and changed their locations and occupations according to the requirements of the labor market, they could eventually find work'.[8] The qualification that only the agent's economic behaviour is being addressed does not obviate the damage done to interpersonal relationships. As Walter Neale has noted,

> a System of Self-Regulating Markets takes a large portion of human activity and sets it aside from all other activity, gives it a set of rules to live by – rules subject to no higher control – and permits the whole of this activity to be governed by the supply–demand–price mechanism. Because economic activities and other aspects of life are closely interrelated, a self-regulating market therefore tends to shape all other activity to a much greater degree than the economy would under other types of economic organization. (*TMEE*, p. 365)

A worker cannot, after all, relocate his employment geographically without moving himself and his family as well. Nor can a movement from one economic sector to another fail to sever interpersonal ties of one kind and other. 'On the social side family unity and community life are put in a constant state of flux since the personnel are so easily forced into movement' (*TMEE*, p. 365). And this mobility of labour, enforced by unemployment and other market sanctions, is a factor of market capitalism, not industrialism. There is nothing in the nature of machine industrial technology that requires it. The salient issues involved are not explicable in terms of technological considerations. They are instead questions of price, cost, and profitability answered by those whose power and interest are vested in the scarcity price system. To be sure, the crucial decisions made are about how technology is employed, and there is some truth behind the common notion that the requirements of machinery are superior to social and human needs. But as Knight makes clear, it is to the requirements of the market economy that one must look to explain the necessity that independent action exist such that social considerations and non-market relations do not interfere with exchange behaviour. In practice, Knight's assumption was expressed in the institutionalization of the freedom of contract, and 'this meant that the non-contractual organizations of kinship, neighborhood, profession, and creed were liquidated since they claimed the allegiance of the individual and thus restrained his freedom' (*GT*, p. 163).

The footloose, almost nomadic character of wage–labour is

mirrored in the effects of the market economy on agriculture. As Marx noted, under market capitalism, agriculture was reorganized and shaped along the lines of capitalist industry.[9] But land, like labour, is far more than a mere factor of production, it is nature itself. Land is not a mere utilitarian fount but is instead saturated with numerous other social functions and meanings (see *GT*, pp. 178 and 184). The point has been forcefully made in a recent book by Wendell Berry. Berry emphasizes the culture in the compound term agriculture, and insists that the organization of farming has profound consequences beyond the production and distribution of foodstuffs and fibres. The questions of body and soul 'are also agricultural, for no matter how urban our life, our bodies live by farming'.[10] In Berry's view, the way people treat their bodies and each other reflects the way they treat the earth and its non-human species; the agriculture of a society is intimately connected with the character of its people. Berry insists that a civilization's social and ecological stability is rooted in its agrarian culture.

> A healthy culture is a communal order of memory, insight, value, work, conviviality, reverence, aspiration. It reveals the human necessities and the human limits. It clarifies our inescapable bonds to the earth and to each other. It assures that the necessary restraints are observed, that necessary work is done, and that it is done well. A healthy *farm* culture can be based only on familiarity and can grow only among a people soundly established upon the land; it nourishes and safeguards a human intelligence of the earth that no amount of technology can satisfactorily replace. The growth of such a culture was once a strong possibility in the farm communities of [the U.S.A.]. We now have only the sad remnants of those communities.[11]

Many of Berry's concerns were noted in a case study published three decades earlier by Walter Goldschmidt.[12] The concern of both men is that agribusiness does not provide the communal and ecological roots that family farming does, and that these roots are essential to a healthy civilization. Once again, society is imperiled by the institutional logic of industrial market capitalism, and once again the critical question is not technology per se but power and control, i.e. institutions for making and implementing decisions.

As the earlier discussion of the three commodity fictions made clear, the market economy is at odds not only with the social and ecological needs of labour and land but also with industrial production itself through the important matter of purchasing power. A system fuelled by profits must have a high degree of monetary stability and yet have a monetary system capable of expanding along with industrial output. 'This is the easily understandable reason why a system of commodity money, such as the market mechanism tends to produce without outside interference, is incompatible with industrial production' (*GT*, p. 193). Commodity money, usually gold or silver, simply cannot be relied upon to expand apace with industrial output. If it does not, a deflation ensues which is ruinous to profits and economic calculation. Token monetary systems result but these in turn conflict with the need for commodity money in international trade. In the nineteenth century, 'in its simplest form, the problem was this: commodity money was vital to the existence of foreign trade; token money, to the existence of domestic trade' (*GT*, p. 193). Central banking, part of the protective response, largely mitigated this conflict, but it did not do so entirely and remnants of the problem still bedevil the managed economies of today. The analysis provided by Thorstein Veblen of the conflict between commerce and industry is further testament to Polanyi's point.

In summary, the true defect of the age was that the market economy allowed the subordination of social and human needs to the requirements of machine efficiency. Everything was subordinated to the paramount necessity of production, including even consumption, as Galbraith has forcefully instructed us. Mass consumption is patterned after the requirements of mass production, i.e. what can be profitably mass produced. Non-market or non-commodity needs, externalities, social wants, and the like have been neglected. The market economy requires a market society which in turn maintains a market personality through a market culture. The personality and character of individuals have been subordinated to the logic of industrial market capitalism. Polanyi was well aware of this, as when he wrote:

> The first century of the Machine Age is drawing to a close. . . . Its fabulous material success was due to the willing, indeed the enthusiastic, subordination of man to the needs of the machine. Liberal capitalism was in effect man's initial response to the challenge of the Industrial Revolution. In order to allow scope to the use of elaborate, powerful machinery, we transformed human

> economy into a self-adjusting system of markets, and cast our thoughts and values in the mold of this unique innovation. (*PAME*, p. 59)

This initial response to industrialism must be, and largely if unconsciously has been, abandoned and 'how to organize human life in a machine society is a question that confronts us anew' (*PAME*, p. 59). For 'if industrialism is not to extinguish the race, it must be subordinated to the requirements of man's nature,' (*GT*, p. 249) 'even though this may mean a technologically less efficient society' (*PAME*, p. 73). Polanyi foresaw the crises now becoming obvious and anticipated the now common prophetry of doom because his historical perspective enabled him to identify the poisonous catalyst in the mix of industrial market capitalism, the myth of the self-regulating market. He recognized too that the struggle was first and foremost ideological, the necessity of overcoming the obsolete market mentality and replacing it with an ideology with which to guide the humane and reasonable administration of the industrial economy.

INDUSTRIALISM AND THE LOGIC OF REFORM

A principal theme which has united American Institutionalism for its century of life is that industrialism contains within itself a logic of reform. This theme was imported to America by the precursors and founders of Institutionalism, men such as Richard T. Ely, Edwin R. A. Seligman, and Henry Carter Adams, who studied in Germany with the German Historicists.[13] The Historicists, in a wide-ranging break with classical economics over method and the nature of economic science, rejected *laissez-faire* and emphasized the potential for state economic action and social reform. The new American political economists acted out of a recognition 'that the industrial revolution . . . had ushered in a host of new problems that . . . had made society so complex that laissez faire was no longer a tenable policy'.[14] Pragmatists and evolutionists, these men, in the words of Richard Mayo-Smith, were 'trying to discover . . . how to adjust institutions more perfectly to human needs'.[15]

I regard this phrase from Mayo-Smith as something of a clarion call for Institutionalism because, other than the methodological dissent from orthodoxy, this reformist bent is very likely the single most important defining characteristic of Institutionalism. As has been pointed out by Allan Gruchy, the principal historian and systematizer of Institutionalist theory, Institutionalism insists that there is a logic of capitalistic industrial development which includes a logic of reform.

> The logic of economic development shows that modern industrial technology is throwing economic activity into a mold which is becoming increasingly collective in nature. This technology, if not interrupted in its development, will continue its work of transforming the competitive economy into a system in which collective economic action is of major importance. The logic of this economic development necessarily leads to some form of intervention by forces which operate outside private markets, since the modern economy cannot function smoothly and efficiently under the direction of private enterprise alone.[16]

The point is again clear: the admixture of industrialism and the market economy generates forces leading to the supersession of the latter.

The Institutionalists proper, as did Polanyi, took a somewhat broader view than the Historicists of the political or administrative process that emerged to displace the self-regulating market economy. For example, Walton Hamilton, in his important book, *The Politics of Industry*, uses politics 'in the Aristotelian sense as an over-all term for the usages and traditions, for the arrangements and policies through which men are governed and through which men – usurping the functions of the gods – attempt to shape destiny'.[17] Hamilton goes on to define industry, in a fashion reminiscent of Polanyi's substantive definition of the economy, as 'the concatenation of interrelated activities which turn out the stream of goods and services out of which men and women, as best they can, fashion their standards of life'. Hamilton's reference to usurping the functions of the gods is significant. He is rejecting any mystified, naturalistic conception of life in favour of humankind's recognizing its own collective responsibility and consciously adopting administrative procedures to structure its life, especially the getting of its livelihood.

The myth of the self-regulating market is, of course, a mystified, even naturalistic construct. The natural law foundation of incipient political and economic liberalism is commonplace and the congruence of market capitalism with human nature is daily reaffirmed in popular, that is to say business, ideology. In his brilliant exposition of the liberal creed, Friedrich Hayek is very explicit about the necessity of submitting to the poorly understood, even arbitrary forces of the market.[18] He argues that twentieth-century democratic society has wrongheadedly transferred the passion to understand and control from natural science and technology to the social realm. A similar plea for trusting the dimly known forces of the market is found in a recent book by a leading figure in the other wing of modern liberalism. Charles Schultze writes about the 'mystery of the market': it works but almost no one knows how it does so.[19] There is no interest here to belittle the considerable achievements of Hayek or Schultze. I use them as representatives of the economics profession to indicate that considerable mystification or obscurantism continues to surround the workings of the market.

Hamilton makes clear his views on the current substance of the self-regulating market concept.

> The thesis here is that the market which of old was sovereign to the whole economy has been deposed, and that the mandate of supply and demand which rigidly it enforced has ceased to be an "iron law." It is not that the market is no longer of importance. . . . It is rather that the throne has had to be shared . . . ; and that the stream of judgments by which the vast network of productive activities is kept going no longer emerges from the automatic play of economic forces. A host of procedures and arrangements – political and character – have invaded the domain of business. As a result there has arisen, quite apart from the ordinary operations of state, a government of industry which in its own distinctive way has its constitution and its statutes, its administrative and judicial processes, and its own manner of dealing with those who do not abide by the law of industry.[20]

The market economy has been deposed because 'as an unleashed force competition is dangerous'. Hamilton emphasizes that the corporation is itself a major force in this deposition. 'Corporate decisions involve discretion, and where there is discretion there is the making of policy, and policy is a political phenomenon.'[21] Accordingly, in the revolutionary deposition of the market economy, it was 'the businessman who among them all was the greatest of radicals'.[22]

Hamilton is quick to point out that the revolutionary deposition of the market economy was not a revolution in the ordinary sense of a programmatic transformation.

> The old order was never absolished. No law, statute, mandate, or decree brought it to an end. There was no intent on anyone's part to set down a period and formally to proclaim a new era. The great transformation – the word is more exact than revolution – came at a headlong pace, and yet was gradual . . .
>
> The new order of things emerged unplanned, unsaluted and unsung. It is not a response to a call for an economic order which is fresh and different. . . . Instead it is a by-product of the everyday concern of a host of individuals with their own problems.[23]

This is, of course, similar to Polanyi's insistence that the protective response was not the result of a leftist conspiracy or ideological shift. Hamilton argues that this transformation has blurred the sharp distinction between public and private that was a key ingredient of the liberal ideology. As Polanyi noted, under the liberal view there was an eclipse of political thinking which allowed, in Hamilton's words, a 'great separation, the state was one sort of thing and the economy quite another'.[24] But in the new order,

> the line between private and public has ceased to be sharply drawn. Yet the breakdown of the separation has not brought union and has not stripped from either the business economy or the political state its own identity. They exist side by side as aspects of, rather than as distinct dominions within, a single culture. Each of the two is still in transition. . . . The problem of their relationship needs an almost continuous restatement.[25]

In Hamilton's view, then, the new order is composed of a private government and a public government. The private government is the sum of the corporations, associations, federations, unions, and other entities which formulate the arrangements and policies by which industry is governed in its day-to-day activities. The two governments interact in a dynamic process of everchanging roles and procedures, each explicitly using the other's mechanisms to secure this or that objective, and the ruling objective matrix in this process is the administration of the economy. It is this dynamism, this shifting of place and function, that makes action under the aegis of the market myth so dysfunctional. Under the eclipse of political thinking, the process of continuous reinterpretation is stymied and tired shibboleths displace new ideas and departures.

Similar themes are found in the words of J. K. Galbraith, in which also are found the most systematic discussion of the new industrial economy. In the face of the imperatives of modern industrial technology, he argues, the market is unreliable with respect to eliciting the necessary response from buyers of industrial products and suppliers of capital, materials, and intermediate goods. The market is therefore superseded by vertical integration, control or contracting and replaced with industrial planning.[26] Galbraith also stresses the blurring of the dichotomy between public and private and the integral relationship between the private and public governments: 'the industrial system will not long be regarded as something apart from government. Rather it will increasingly be seen as part of a much larger complex which embraces both the industrial system and the state'.[27]

Galbraith also insists upon the non-ideological nature of the supersession of the market and follows Hamilton in citing business as 'the greatest of radicals' in this great transformation.

> And all who were subject to insecurity sooner or later set about eliminating it as it affected themselves. In large measure they were successful. The devices by which they did so have varied much. This has led those who were using one device to see it as a necessary precaution while they deplored the iniquitous measures devised by others . . .
>
> The elimination of economic insecurity was pioneered by the business firm in respect of its own operations. The greatest source of insecurity . . . lay in competition and the free and unpredictable movement of competitive market prices. From the very beginning of modern capitalist society, businessmen have addressed themselves to the elimination or the mitigation of this source of insecurity.[28]

It is not difficult to find in the Institutionalist literature agreement with Polanyi that the root problem is not industrialism per se but industrial market capitalism. Veblen's celebrated dichotomy between industrial and pecuniary interests is to the point and requires no comment. Mitchell too emphasized the warping of personalities by the pecuniary culture and emphasized that although 'for the well-being of the community efficient industry and commerce [distributive services] are vastly more important than successful money-making . . . , in practice, [they] are thoroughly subordinated to business'.[29] Tugwell also spoke very clearly on this point. 'The conspicuous failure of industrialism is not in what we ordinarily call technique . . . . [but in that] our technique is used not for its intended purpose but for quite another one: not to furnish us an efficiently functioning system, but to establish conditions in which businessmen shall dominate regardless of the costs to everyone else.'[30] Clark's analysis was even closer to Polanyi's than the other Institutionalists. Gruchy, summarizing the final section of Clark's *Studies in the Economics of Overhead Costs*, attributes to Clark the view that 'the industrial system has evolved along lines which may be regarded more as adjustments to the requirements of the machine than as adjustments to the needs of decent human living' owing to the fact that 'the making of the policies that dominate the machine process is restricted to the select few who own or control the machines'.[31] In general, then, for the Institutionalists, the key problem with industrialism to date has been that 'pecuniary considerations are more decisive with respect to the working of the economy than are technological considerations',[32] and the challenge posed by industrialism to a humane civilization cannot be met without first throwing off the mental shackles of the market myth. This is the key theme of Galbraith's work as well. The needs of the corporate 'industrial system' dominate popular attitudes, policy, education, etc.,[33] and the 'imagery of choice' maintained by the market myth and its crony, the neoclassical model, block efforts to reverse this situation.[34]

The Institutionalist literature on industrialism and the logic of reform is the major intellectual effort to provide a *positive* interpretation of the corporate–welfare state. The Institutionalists were probably the first to call attention to the emerging new order which is neither market captalist nor socialist by and large but is instead a hybrid or mixed economy. This theme runs throughout Gruchy's examination of the major Institutionalists in *Modern Economic Thought* and has been emphasized by later writers in the tradition as well, notably Galbraith. The purpose of this brief review is not only to show the consistency of Polanyi's analysis with this body of literature which is the major attempt to interpret the logic of reform but also to suggest the potency of Polanyi's focus on this reform. This focus is of course the contrast between the historical and anthropological norm of the embedded or administered economy and the disembedded economy of market capitalism. The logic of reform is none other than the protective response; the institutional logic at work is the necessity of protecting society against the vagaries of the self-regulating market by reimbedding economic decisions in the social and political fabric.

These myriad reimbedding actions expand in the history of market capitalism because the market mechanism extends its reach and because the growth of scale and complexity of machine industrial technology increases the mayhem wrought by irresponsible market-oriented actions. 'The more comprehensive the market system became, the more it revealed its incapacity to satisfy the requirements of a stable society' (*LM*, p. 1). The tendency of the market toward extension of its reach is commonplace. Market capitalism grew by reaching into and destroying the traditional economy and replacing production for direct use with commodity production. This is an ongoing process. Early in this century, as more of the fabrication and processing of drugs, foodstuffs, and the like were removed from the household to the commodity sphere, regulatory measures were required to protect consumers. More recently, care for children and the elderly have been in process of commoditization. Predictably, it has been necessary to provide protection through regulation of day-care centres and nursing homes. Provision of these services on a commodity basis is far different from their provision through the extended family because in the latter the element of embeddedness remains in the form of the familial relationship.

No matter the means employed, the upshot of the protective response to reimbed the market in society is, of course, the demise of the self-regulating market.

> [W]e are witnessing a development under which the economic system ceases to lay down the law to society and the primacy of society over that system is secured. This may happen in a great variety of ways, democratic and aristocratic, constitutionalist and authoritarian, perhaps even in a fashion yet utterly unforeseen. The future in some countries may be already the present in others, while some may still embody the past of the rest. But the outcome is common with them all: the market system will no longer be self-regulating, even in principle, since it will not comprise labor, land, and money. (*GT*, p. 251)

Polanyi is quick to point out that the demise of the self-regulating market does not portend the disappearance of markets. The market mechanism will no doubt persist and be of enduring instrumentality 'to ensure the freedom of the consumer, to indicate the shifting of demând, to influence producers' income, and to serve as an instrument of accountancy, while ceasing altogether to be an organ of economic self-regulation' (*GT*, p. 252). The piecemeal, even halting nature of the protective response notwithstanding, it is veritably a great transformation and it is not 'the first time in history [that] makeshifts contain the germs of great and permanent institutions' (*GT*, p. 251).

Polanyi's reference to the great variety of ways this transformation *may* be effected does not mean it is a matter of indifference how it is done. Far from it. The manner in which the transformation is finally completed and the market economy cast away in fact and principle is absolutely crucial with respect to the continuation of a humane and civilized way of life. The collapse of the market economy can be replaced with an administered economy placed anywhere along the spectrum between democracy and totalitarianism. The issues come down to retaining and revitalizing the liberal ideals of personal freedom and responsibility while administering the economy to safeguard the reproduction and stability of society. Hence, I now turn to the matter of planning and freedom.

PLANNING AND FREEDOM

For fruitful discussion of the role of the state and individual freedom, it is first necessary to overcome the narrow view of freedom as the absence of state intervention in the market. Preoccupation with this narrow conception has confined the liberal tradition to the conclusion that any expansion in the role of the state is necessarily a decrease in freedom. This myopic perspective is rooted historically in the liberal conception of the market economy as a natural order of some sort which emerged spontaneously due to its superior consonance with human nature. As discussed in Chapter 4 above, Polanyi gave a detailed rebuttal of this view, arguing in effect, that the market economy was a conscious political creation and did not and would not have emerged spontaneously. The importance of this recognition that the market economy resulted from political action, albeit virtually suicidal action for the polity, is to demystify or denaturalize the market economy and take away the aura of inevitability which is its predominant ideological defence. Thusly viewed, market capitalism has no pride of place and the political action of human beings to install it can be examined on equal footing with like action to dismantle it.

Once this intellectual clarification is completed, the problem of freedom must be examined in an altogether different light. Polanyi spoke of 'freedom in a complex society' (*GT*, ch. 21) to underscore the necessity of going beyond the simplism of the market myth. It is simplistic to see freedom primarily in terms of the state's non-interference in market activities and this simplism follows from the image of economy and society contained in the market myth. It is grossly simplistic – not simpleminded since the market myth has been given very sophisticated and artful promulgation – to reduce the economy to a process of calculation and exchange operating to establish relative prices which determine production and distribution, and then to cordon off this sphere as the economy, a thing apart from the polity, family, religion, etc. In reality, the interaction involved is continuous, complex, and commanding so that holistic economic thought is required if the primacy of society is not to be neglected. Because this neglect of society is a threat to freedom, the simplistic market view of freedom is in fact a threat to freedom. Therefore, 'we cannot achieve the freedom we seek, unless we comprehend the true significance of freedom in a complex society' (*GT*, p. 254).

The first step toward treating freedom as a vastly more complicated problem than that envisaged by the market myth is to recognize that there are many different kinds of freedom, some having good effects, some bad. The interaction between the various freedoms are complex. Some freedoms reinforce and strengthen other freedoms while some undermine and threaten other freedoms.

> The breakdown of market economy imperils two kinds of freedoms: some good, some bad.
>
> That the freedom to exploit one's fellows, or the freedom to make inordinate gains without commensurate service to the community, the freedom to keep technological inventions from being used for the public benefit, or the freedom to profit from public calamities secretly engineered for private advantage, may disappear, together with the free market, is all to the good. But the market economy under which these freedoms throve also produced freedoms that we prize highly. Freedom of conscience,

> freedom of speech, freedom of meeting, freedom of association, freedom to choose one's job – we cherish them for their own sake. Yet to a large extent they were by-products of the same economy that was also responsible for the evil freedoms.
>
> The existence of a separate economic sphere in society created, as it were, a gap between politics and economics, between government and industry, that was in the nature of a no man's land. (*PAME*, pp. 74–5)

In this 'no man's land' or institutional lacuna, there flowered the evil and cherished freedoms. In this lacuna also arose the threat to society: 'The institutional separation of politics and economics, which proved a deadly danger to the substance of society, almost automatically produced freedom at the cost of justice and security' (*GT*, pp. 254–5). But a society whose freedoms are purchased at the cost of injustice and insecurity is neither enduring nor good. The problem of democratic control of the economy to protect society is to separate the two kinds of freedoms in order to eliminate the one and preserve the other. This can only be done if the complexity of freedom is recognized and the distinctions among freedoms accepted. 'On the institutional level, regulation both extends and restricts freedom; only the balance of the freedoms lost and won is significant' (*GT*, p. 254).

It is clear from the above that Polanyi conceded to the liberal's insistence that the market economy is linked historically with social and political freedoms. But he sharply dissented from the logical extension that the demise of the market economy must necessarily extinguish all freedom in its wake, i.e. that the evil freedoms are the necessary costs of the cherished ones. There is no necessary abnegation of freedom in a planned economy. 'In truth, we will have just as much freedom as we will desire to create and to safeguard. There is no *one* determinant in human society. Institutional guarantees of personal freedom are compatible with any economic system' (*PAME*, p. 76). The market economy is not a necessary condition for the cherished freedoms.

Indeed, the market economy may not even be a sufficient condition nor even a passive or permissive one. The evil freedoms of the market economy pose a threat to the cherished freedoms. 'It appears that the means of maintaining freedom are themselves adulterating and destroying it' (*GT*, p. 254). The freedoms championed by the liberal thus threaten the liberal's overarching value. This is because the liberal has the narrow, simplistic view of freedom already noted. 'With the liberal the idea of freedom . . . degenerates into a mere advocacy of free enterprise . . .'. (*GT*, p. 257), and it is precisely in free enterprise that one finds the locus of the evil, threatening freedoms. The freedoms of free enterprise are those allowing the irresponsible actions that J. M. Clark wrote of in such passionate terms when he contrasted the reality of the twentieth-century economy to the market conception.

> We have inherited an economics of irresponsibility. We are in an economy of control with which our intellectual inheritance fits but awkwardly. To make control really tolerable we need something more; something which is still in its infancy. We need an economics of responsibility, developed and embodied in our working business ethics.[35]

In contrast to the responsibility needed for a controlled economy,

> the laissez-faire economics may well be characterized as the economics of irresponsibility, and the business system of free contract is also a system of irresponsibility when judged by the same standard. . . . Liberal economics . . . [neglects the responsibility problem] by separating business sharply off from the rest of life.[36]

Clark goes on to denounce the socialization pattern which induces people in business or politics to subscribe to 'the law of getting all they can'. For Clark, 'the economics of control is at war with the economics of irresponsibility'.

E. F. Schumacher also noted the essential element of irresponsibility in the market economy and the shallow, narrow view of human life held out by its ethos.

> The market therefore represents only the surface of society and its significance relates to the momentary situation as it exists there and then. There is no probing into the depths of things, into the natural or social facts that lie behind them. In a sense, the market is the institutionalization of individualism and non-responsibility. Neither buyer nor seller is responsible for anything but himself. It would be "uneconomic" for a wealthy seller to reduce his prices to poor customers merely because they are in need, or for a wealthy

buyer to pay an extra price merely because the supplier is poor. Equally, it would be "uneconomic" for a buyer to give preference to home-produced goods if imported goods are cheaper.[37]

Clearly, Schumacher is referring to disembedded economic decisions made without due consideration of social or political factors. Schumacher also notes a key point made by Polanyi: 'What may cause surprise is that it is also considered virtuous to make the maximum use of this freedom from responsibility.' Irresponsible self-seeking is not merely present, but expected and legitimate.

Certainly no one has excelled Veblen in making the case that sharp practice and irresponsible action are not incidental but the heart and core of the market capitalist economy. The freedom of free enterprise – the 'rule of self-help and free bargaining' – is the right to wreck matters at large in the pursuit of one's self-interest. The essential power of private property in such a setting is not to hold for personal use but rather to withhold from social use if one is dissatisfied with the terms of the bargain.

> [A]ny person who has a legal right to withhold any part of the necessary industrial apparatus or materials from current use will be in a position to impose terms and exact obedience, on pain of rendering the community's joint stock of technology inoperative to that extent. Ownership of industrial equipment and natural resources confers such a right legally to enforce unemployment, and so to make the community's workmanship useless to that extent.[38]

It follows that one's power to command income in the normal operation of market capitalism is directly related to the mayhem one can wreak by refusing to cooperate, i.e. by the derangement of the social process of production that one can cause.

> The common good, so far as it is a question of material welfare, is evidently best served by an unhampered working of the industrial system . . . without interruption or dislocation. But it is equally evident that the owner or manager of any given concern or section of this industrial system may be in a position to gain something for himself at the cost of the rest by obstructing, retarding or dislocating this working system at some critical point in such a way as will enable him to get the best of the bargain in

> his dealings with the rest. This appears constantly in the altogether usual, and altogether legitimate, practice of holding out for a better price. So also in the scarcely less usual, and no less legitimate, practice of withholding needed ground or right of way, or needed materials or information, from a business rival. . . . All these things are usual and a matter of course, because business management under [present] conditions . . . is in great part made up of these things. Sabotage of this kind is indispensable to any large success in industrial business.[39]

As a result, a radical disjuncture exists between the interests of society and those practising businesslike management of their property. 'The outcome of this management of industrial affairs through pecuniary transactions, therefore, has been to dissociate the interests of those men who exercise the discretion from the interests of the community.'[40] Veblen had earlier pointed out that an important root of this happenstance was the transition to profit-seeking business management in capitalism, in contrast to the 'pre-capitalistic business situation [in which] business . . . was customarily managed with a view to earning a livelihood rather than with a view to profits on investment'.[41] This is, of course, Aristotle's distinction between natural and unnatural exchange, upon which Polanyi placed so much emphasis.

These freedoms of irresponsible self-seeking and sharp practice threaten all freedoms because they threaten society. By creating injustice, insecurity, and disorder, they leave the way open to an authoritarian, totalitarian resolution. The primacy of society exists, it is reality, and social reproduction, i.e. the continuation of society, will be achieved by measures as extreme and dire as deemed necessary. Without a viable resolution of the problem of freedom and order in a free society, the issue will be settled all on the side of order. The fascistic regimes of the early twentieth century arose from just such disorder created by a stalemate of irresponsible forces clashing in industry and government in a polarized political economy.

> Under conditions such as these the routine conflict of interests . . . took on an ominous character. While a divergence of economic interests would normally end in compromise, the separation of the economic and political spheres in society tended to invest such clashes with grave consequences to the community.

> . . . A clash of group interests that resulted in paralyzing the organs of industry or state – either of them, or both – formed an immediate peril to society.
>
> [T]his was the case in the twenties. . . . Eventually, the moment would come when both the economic and political systems were threatened by complete paralysis. Fear would grip the people, and leadership would be thrust upon those who offered an easy way out at whatever ultimate price. The time was ripe for the fascist solution. (*GT*, pp. 235–6)

The problem is not only one of crisis-ridden, short-sighted pragmatism; it has a philosophical or theoretical level as well. Viewing freedom simplistically, the liberal attacks 'planning and control . . . as a denial of freedom' (*GT*, p. 257). In so doing, the liberal neglects the primacy of society and the reality that power and compulsion are necessary for any functioning social order. 'The function of power is to ensure that measure of conformity which is needed for the survival of the group . . .' (*GT*, p. 258). The essential flaw in the liberal logic is the eclipse of political thinking, which Polanyi regarded as the key intellectual deficiency of the liberal era (see *LM*, pp. 15–17). Politics and its role in society was lost sight of in the scramble to interpret social organization in a manner consistent with the needs of the market economy. Historical and anthropological accounts of pre-market economies became nonsensical because the true functions of the polity became invisible with the spread of economistic thinking. The vital role of the polity in institutionalizing and controlling economic behaviour and in upholding social ideals was neglected. The liberal's naïveté about economic motives is matched only by his cynicism about political motives.

By defining freedom as the absence of such control, a control which is vitally necessary to the continuation of society, the liberal opens the way for the fascist denial of freedom. 'The fascist answer to the recognition of the reality of society is the rejection of the postulate of freedom' (*GT*, p. 258A). Liberal simplism is defenceless against this conclusion because any 'ideal that would ban power and compulsion from society is intrinsically invalid' (*PAME*, p. 74).

> Freedom's utter frustration in fascism is, indeed, the inevitable result of the liberal philosophy, which claims that power and compulsion are evil, that freedom demands their absence from a human community. No such thing is possible; in a complex society

> this becomes apparent. This leaves no alternative but either to remain faithful to an illusionary idea of freedom and deny the reality of society, or accept that reality and reject the idea of freedom. The first is the liberal's conclusion; the later the fascist's. No other seems possible. (*GT*, p. 257)

This dilemma is more apparent that real; it is the creation of the liberal illusion concerning power and compulsion.

> No society is possible in which power and compulsion are absent, nor a world in which force has no function. . . . Yet this [illusion] was the result of a market-view of society which equated economics with contractual relationships, and contractual relations with freedom. . . . Vision was limited by the market which "fragmented" life into the producers' sector that ended when his product reached the market, and the sector of the consumer for whom all goods sprang from the market. The one derived his income "freely" from the market, the other spent it "freely" there. Society as a whole remained invisible. The power of the State was of no account, since the less its power the smoother the market mechanism would function. Neither voters, nor owners, neither producers, nor consumers could be held responsible for such brutal restrictions of freedom as were involved in the occurrence of unemployment and destitution. Any decent individual could imagine himself free from all responsibility for acts of compulsion on the part of a State which he, personally, rejected; or for economic suffering in society from which he, personally, had not benefited. He was "paying his way," was "in nobody's debt," and was unentangled in the evil of power and economic value. His lack of responsibility for them seemed so evident that he denied their reality in the name of his freedom.
>
> But power and economic value are a paradigm of social reality . . . . (*GT*, pp. 257–8)

The way out of the dilemma is to overcome the eclipse of political thinking inherent in the narrow purview of economistic liberalism, recognize the primacy of society and the necessary political constraint and molding of economic activity, and build a viable concept of freedom upon this recognition. Only such a realistic, social view of freedom can be made defensible against the totalitarian denial.

Armed with a view that both recognizes the reality of society, i.e.

the necessity of power and compulsion, and insists upon the possibility of freedom in a complex society, the denizens of industrialism can move on to consider the appropriate ways of administering the economy through some form of democratic planning. The task, as already noted, is to institute planning in such a way as to preserve the cherished freedoms of the market era and eliminate the evil ones, at the same time securing reasonable efficiency, economic stability, and social justice. In effect, the objective of planning is to secure through conscious, concerted social action much of what the market myth claims to be the natural outcome of the self-regulating market economy.

> We must try to maintain by all means in our power these high values inherited from the market economy which collapsed. This, assuredly, is a great task. Neither freedom nor peace could be institutionalized under that economy, since its purpose was to create profits and welfare, not peace and freedom. We will have consciously to strive for them in the future if we are to possess them at all; they must become chosen aims of the societies towards which we are moving. (*GT*, p. 255)

Polanyi was insistent that special care should be taken to preserve and extend personal liberty, which

> will exist to the degree in which we will deliberately create new safeguards for its maintenance and, indeed, extension . . .
>
> Every move toward integration in society should thus be accompanied by an increase of freedom; moves towards planning should comprise the strengthening of the rights of the individual in society. . . . The true answer to the threat of bureaucracy as a source of abuse of power is to create spheres of arbitrary freedom protected by unbreakable rules. . . . No mere declaration of rights can suffice: institutions are required to make the rights effective. (*GT*, pp. 255–6)

Polanyi noted that these protective measures should include the bureaucracies of the private government as well as the nominal state and that new rights should be added to the Bill of Rights, beginning with protection of one's job against discrimination and subtle victimization. And, to this vital task of 'vindicating personal freedom', a back seat should be taken by efficient production, abundant consumption, and rational administration. Given this moral and institutional commitment, and without it a populace cannot be free in any event, Polanyi feared neither planning nor power.

> Uncomplaining acceptance of the reality of society gives man indomitable courage and strength to remove all removable injustice and unfreedom. As long as he is true to his task of creating more abundant freedom for all, he need not fear that either power or planning will turn against him and destroy the freedom he is building by their instrumentality. This is the meaning of freedom in a complex society . . . . (*GT*, p. 258B)

Industrialism then makes possible an increase in freedom due to the tremendous advance it brings in mankind's substantive and technological power. But its imperatives and mass society also threaten freedom and 'the danger to liberty lies in the subordination of belief to the needs of the industrial system'.[42] To avert this peril, the forces of industrialism must be humanized through a sound understanding of the place and function of the economy in society. This understanding indicates the necessity of control or regimentation of the forces of industrialism. 'Regimentation of material and mechanical forces is the only way by which the mass of individuals can be released from regimentation and consequent suppression of their cultural possibilities.'[43] The irresponsibility of market society is not a viable freedom because freedom cannot survive on the basis of a destruction of society.

> The passing of market economy can become the beginning of an era of unprecedented freedom. Juridical and actual freedom can be made much wider and more general than ever before; regulation and control can achieve freedom not only for the few, but for all. Freedom not as an appurtenance of privilege, tainted at the source, but as a prescriptive right extending far beyond the narrow confines of the political sphere into the intimate organization of society itself. Thus will old freedoms and civic rights be added to the fund of new freedom generated by the leisure and security that industrial society offers to all. Such a society can afford to be both just and free. (*GT*, p. 256)

Not just any form of control is adequate to the task. Mere

intervention is not planning, and the mere accumulation of rules and regulations and politicized economic relationships will not achieve an administered economy in which personal liberties and other human values are safeguarded. Nor is just any form of planning acceptable; it must be participatory, institutionalized in such a way as to encourage the widest possible popular input and understanding. Planning must be a learning process in which people are moved to learn about the economy, its place in society, and its relation to their lives.[44] It was this 'bottom up' planning that Polanyi desired; he rejected any 'topdown' scenario.

> Among those in America who are aware of the dimensions of the problem, two tendencies are discernible: some believe in elites and aristocracies, in managerialism and the corporation. They feel that the whole of society should be more intimately adjusted to the economic system, which they would wish to remain unchanged. This is the ideal of the Brave New World, where the individual is conditioned to support an order that has been designed for him by such as are wiser than he. Others, on the contrary, believe that in a truly democratic society, the problem of industry would resolve itself through the planned intervention of the producers and consumers themselves. Such conscious and responsible action is, indeed, one of the embodiments of freedom in a complex society. But . . . such an endeavor cannot be successful unless it is disciplined by a total view of man and society very different from that which we inherited from market economy. (*PAME*, pp. 76–7)

The reference to 'conscious and responsible action' disciplined by a new view of man and society indicates that planning cannot be made to work if it is merely superimposed on the market society with the personality structures of individuals of that society. The social psychology of planning is of crucial importance. The new order of planning must include institutions leading to a revivified *civitas* and *philia*; it must pave the way for values articulation and clarification as well as resolution of values conflicts.

In the final analysis, then, the problem of freedom is part of a much larger problem set.

> The question of individual freedom . . . is only one aspect of this anxious problem. In truth, it forms part of a much wider and

> deeper need – the need for a new response to the total challenge of the machine.
>
> Our condition may be described in these terms: Industrial civilization may yet undo man. But since the venture of a progressively artificial environment cannot, will not, and indeed, should not, be voluntarily discarded, the task of adapting life *in such a surrounding* to the requirements of human existence must be resolved if man is to continue on earth. No one can foretell whether such an adjustment is possible, or whether man must perish in the attempt. Hence the dark undertone of concern. (*PAME*, p. 60)

It is clear that the market economy cannot preserve a humane existence in the face of industrialism and that it is necessary to reimbed the economy in society through an administered and communitized economy. If indeed the corporate–welfare state is the solution to the riddle posed by industrialism, then a positive theory of this response is needed in order to realize its promise. If it is not the solution, then the same intellectual effort is required in order to establish both its shortcomings and institutional alternatives. This is after all, the responsibility of the intellectual, to forge the concepts necessary to permit alternative institutional frameworks to come into view.

In summary, the greatest threat to freedom is a poorly instituted administered economy, such as must exist so long as democratic industrial society labours under the influence of the market mentality. In practice, society has rejected Hayek's call for submission to the organic process of uncontrolled market forces with its attendant windfall gains and losses, insecurity, instability, and unmanaged change. Conscious social control of the forces which shape life chances and their realization is a powerful popular commitment. The task ahead is to throw off the ideological remnant of the nineteenth century, the market mentality, so to be able to construct a theory with which to inform and guide the practice to which democratic industrial society is committed.

Notes

1 THE LIFE AND WORK OF KARL POLANYI

1. I rely not only on published sources for this biographical synopsis but also upon conversations and correspondence with those who knew Polanyi. I am particularly indebted to a lengthy response from Kari Polanyi-Levitt to an initial draft. The sources I have used, in addition to the book notes on Polanyi's publications, are as follows: Ilona Ducyznska Polanyi, 'Karl Polanyi: Notes on His Life', *LM*, pp. xi–xx; Kari Levitt, 'Karl Polanyi and "Co-Existence"', *Co-Existence*, 1 (Nov. 1964) pp. 113–21; Paul Bohannon and George Dalton, 'Karl Polanyi: 1886–1964', *American Anthropologist*, 67 (Dec. 1965) pp. 1508–11; Hans Zeisel, 'Polanyi, Karl', in David L. Sills (ed.), *International Encyclopedia of the Social Sciences*, vol. 12 (New York: Macmillan, 1968) pp. 172–4; Peter F. Drucker, *Adventures of a Bystander* (New York: Harper & Row, 1978) pp. 123–40; Lee Congdon, 'Karl Polanyi in Hungary, 1900–19', *Journal of Contemporary History*, 11 (Jan. 1976) pp. 167–83; S. C. Humphreys, 'History, Economics, and Anthropology: the Work of Karl Polanyi', *History and Theory*, 8, No. 2 (1969) pp. 165–212; Eva Fekete and Eva Karadi (eds), *Gyorgy Lukacs: His Life in Pictures and Documents* (Budapest: Coivina Kiado, 1981); and Fred Block and Margaret R. Somers, 'Beyond the Economistic Fallacy: the Holistic Social Science of Karl Polanyi', in Theda Skocpol (ed.), *Broad Visions: Methods of Historical Social Analysis* (New York: Cambridge University Press, forthcoming). Ilona Ducyznska, *Workers in Arms* (*Monthly Review*, New York, 1978) is a useful background work on the interwar political culture in which Polanyi lived.
2. Quoted in Congdon, 'Polanyi in Hungary', p. 173.
3. Quoted in ibid.
4. 'Sozialistische Rechnungslegung', *Archiv für Sozialwissenschaft*, 49 (1922) 377–420.
5. Levitt, 'Karl Polanyi and "Co-Existence"', p. 118.
6. Polanyi, *Biographical Notes* (unpublished c. 1963); quoted in ibid., p. 116.
7. Polanyi, ibid.
8. See J. O. Appleby, *Economic Thought and Ideology in Seventeenth Century England* (Princeton University Press, 1978).
9. Steuart, *An Inquiry into the Principles of Political Oeconomy*, vol. 1, (London: 1767) p. 16.
10. See William Appleman Williams, *The Contours of American History*

(New York: Franklin Watts, 1973) pp. 32–61; and, James Clark Sherburne, *John Ruskin, or the Ambiguities of Abundance* (Cambridge: Harvard University Press, 1972) p. 107.

11. Polanyi, quoted in Congdon, 'Polanyi in Hungary', p. 179.
12. For a contrast of methodological essentialism and nominalism, see Karl R. Popper, *The Open Society and its Enemies* (Princeton University Press, 1950) pp. 34–5. Interestingly, Popper in that work (p. 485) recounts a 1925 discussion with Polanyi on the merits of the two methodological orientations for the social sciences. As I make clear in the test, I interpret Polanyi's debate with essentialism to be more that of an existentialist than a positivist thinker.
13. See Trevor Smith, *The Politics of the Corporate Economy* (London: Martin Robertson, 1979) part I.
14. Compare *The Great Transformation* to F. A. Hayek, *The Road to Serfdom* (University of Chicago Press, 1944).
15. 'History, Economics and Anthropology', p. 174.
16. George H. Hildebrand, Jr, *American Economic Review* 36 (June 1946) 398–405.
17. George Dalton and Jasper Köcke, 'The Work of the Polanyi Group: Past, Present, and Future', paper presented at a conference on economic anthropology, Indiana University, Bloomington, Indiana, Apr. 1981.
18. The formalist-substantivist controversy of the 1960s was a new round in an ongoing debate about the relation between anthropology and economics. Bronislaw Malinowski, Marcel Mauss, D. M. Goodfellow, Melville Herskovits, and Frank Knight were among the participants in this earlier discussion. See Knight, 'Anthropology and Economics', *Journal of Political Economy*, 49 (Apr. 1941) 247–68; Herskovits, 'Anthropology and Economics: a Rejoinder', *Journal of Political Economy*, 49 (Apr. 1941) 269–78; Raymond Firth (ed.), *Themes in Economic Anthropology* (London: Tavistock, 1967); and, Jasper Köcke, 'Some Early German Contributions to Economic Anthropology', in George Dalton (ed.), *Research in Economic Anthropology*, vol. II (Greenwich, Conn.: JAI Press, 1979) pp. 119–67.

    The Polanyi round of the debate was touched off by George Dalton's expression of Polanyi's views in 'Economic Theory and Primitive Society', *American Anthropologist*, 63 (Feb. 1961) 1–25. There followed a series of articles in that journal: Robbins Burling, 'Maximization Theories in the Study of Economic Anthropology', 64 (Sept. 1962) 802–21; Edward E. LeClair, 'Economic Theory and Economic Anthropology', 64 (Dec. 1962) 1179–203; and Scott Cook, 'The Obsolete "Antimarket" Mentality: a Critique of the Substantive Approach to Economic Anthropology', 68 (Apr. 1966) 323–45. For an assessment of the controversy by Dalton, see 'Theoretical Issues in Economic Anthropology', *Current Anthropology* 10 (Feb. 1969) 63–101. See also David Kaplan, 'The Formalist–Substantivist Controversy in Economic Anthropology', *Southwestern Journal of Anthropology*, 24 (Autumn 1968) 228–47; and, John H. Dowling, 'The Goodfellows vs. the Dalton Gang: the Assumptions of Economic Anthropology', *Journal of Anthropological Research*, 35 (1979) 292–308.

19. See Anne Mayhew, 'Atomistic and Cultural Analyses in Economic Anthropology: an Old Argument Repeated', in John Adams (ed.), *Institutional Economics: Essays in Honor of Allen G. Gruchy* (Boston: Martinus Nijhoff, 1980) pp. 72–81.
20. See Humphreys, 'History, Economics and Anthropology', pp. 198–9.
21. This was a large part of Polanyi's break with the economic determinism of the Marxist Second International. See Block and Somers, 'Beyond the Economistic Fallacy'.
22. See Marvin Harris, 'The Economy Has No Surplus?', *American Anthropologist*, 61 (Feb. 1959) 185–99; George Dalton, 'A Note of Clarification on Economic Surplus', *American Anthropologist*, 62 (June 1960) 482–90; and 'Economic Surplus, Once Again', *American Anthropologist* (1963) 389–94. See also I. Sachs, 'La Notion de Surplus et son Application aux Economies Primitives', *L'Homme*, 6 (1966) 5–18.
23. See Jacques Melitz, 'The Polanyi School of Anthropology on Money: an Economist's View', *American Anthropologist*, 70 (Oct. 1970) 1020–40; George Dalton, 'Primitive Money', *American Anthropologist*, 67 (1965) 44–65; Walter C. Neale, *Monies in Societies* (San Francisco: Chandler & Sharp, 1976); and, Philip Grierson, 'The Origins of Money', in George Dalton (ed.), *Research in Economic Anthropology*, vol. I (Greenwich, Conn.: JAI Press, 1978) 1–35.
24. See, for example, Richard Hodges, 'Ports of Trade in Early Medieval Europe', *Norwegian Archaeological Review*, 11 (1978) 97–101; and, Clifford Geertz, 'Ports of Trade in Nineteenth Century Bali', in George Dalton (ed.), *Research in Economic Anthropology*, vol. III, (Greenwich, Conn.: JAI Press, 1980).
25. See the discussion in George Dalton (ed.), *Research in Economic Anthropology*, vol. IV (Greenwich, Conn.: JAI Press, 1981) 1–93.
26. See Kenneth E. Boulding, *The Economy of Love and Fear* (Belmont, Calif.: Wadsworth, 1978) pp. 25–30.
27. See Humphreys, 'History, Economics and Anthropology', pp. 178–82; M. I. Finley, *The Ancient Economy* (Berkeley: University of California Press, 1973); Douglass C. North, 'Markets and Other Allocation Systems in History: the Challenge of Karl Polanyi', *Journal of European Economic History*, 6 (Winter 1977) 703–16; and, E. L. Jones, *The European Miracle* (New York: Cambridge University Press, 1981). See also Irma Adelman and Cynthia Taft Morris, 'Patterns of Market Expansion in the Nineteenth Century: a Quantitative Study', in Dalton (ed.), *Research in Economic Anthropology*, vol. I, pp. 231–4.
28. Appleby, *Economic Thought and Ideology*.
29. See Block and Somers, 'Beyond the Economistic Fallacy'.
30. See ibid.
31. See Alan Sievers, *Has Market Capitalism Collapsed?* (New York: Columbia University Press, 1949); and 'On Karl Polanyi', lecture at Colorado State University, Apr. 1977; and, David Hamilton, 'The Great Wheel of Wealth', *American Journal of Economics and Sociology*, 24 (July 1965) 241–48. In addition, a younger generation of institutional

economists is actively studying Polanyi's works and can be expected to make contributions displaying his influence in the near future.

32. Arthur M. Okun, *Equality and Efficiency* (Washington, DC: Brookings Institution, 1975) p. 12; and, Charles Kindleberger, 'Review of *The Great Transformation*', *Daedalus*, 103 (1974) 45–52.
33. Paul Medow, 'The Humanistic Ideals of the Enlightenment and Mathematical Economics', in Erich Fromm (ed.), *Socialist Humanism* (Garden City, NJ: Anchor Books, 1966) pp. 405–17.
34. This is from a 1913 article that Polanyi published in Hungarian, as quoted by Congdon, 'Polanyi in Hungary', p. 174.
35. Karl Polanyi, 'Hamlet', *Yale Review, New Series*, 43 (Mar. 1954) p. 349.
36. Polanyi, quoted from an unpublished 1960 manuscript by Levitt, 'Karl Polanyi and "Co-Existence"', p. 113.
37. Polanyi, 'Hamlet', p. 339.
38. Ibid., p. 350.
39. Polanyi, 1960, as quoted by Levitt, 'Karl Polanyi and "Co-Existence"', p. 114.
40. Ibid., p. 114.

2 THE METHODOLOGY OF ECONOMICS

1. Karl Marx, *Grundrisse* (New York: Vintage, 1973) p. 105.
2. Lynn White, Jr, *Medieval Technology and Social Change* (New York: Oxford University Press, 1964) pp. 5, 10, and 28.
3. Marx, *Grundrisse*, p. 83.
4. See K. William Kapp, *The Social Costs of Private Enterprise* (New York: Schocken, 1971) pp. 255–62.
5. See J. Ron Stanfield, *Economic Thought and Social Change* (Carbondale: Southern Illinois University Press, 1979).
6. This example is taken from Adolph Lowe, *On Economic Knowledge*, enlarged edn (White Plains, New York: M. E. Sharpe, 1977).
7. Lionel, Lord Robbins, *An Essay on the Nature and Significance of Economic Science*, 2nd edn (New York: St. Martin's, 1969) p. 12.
8. Ibid., p. 17.
9. Marshall Sahlins, *Stone Age Economics* (Chicago: Aldine, 1972) p. 186n.
10. See, e.g. the review of American Historicists in Sidney Fine, *Laissez Faire and the General–Welfare State* (Ann Arbor: University of Michigan Press, 1964) ch. VII.
11. See Stanfield, *Economic Thought*, ch. 7.
12. Robbins, *Economic Science*, p. 7.
13. Alfred North Whitehead, *Science and the Modern World* (New York: 1925), quoted by Talcott Parsons, 'Wants and Activities in Marshall', *Quarterly Journal of Economics*, 46 (Nov. 1931) p. 101.
14. Whitehead, *Process and Reality* (New York, 1929) p. 11, quoted by

Nicholas Georgescu-Roegen, *The Entropy Law and the Economic Process* (Cambridge: Harvard University Press, 1971) p. 321.
15. J. A. Schumpeter, *History of Economic Analysis* (New York: Oxford University Press, 1954) pp. 473, 668, and 1171.
16. Whitehead, *Science and the Modern World*, p. 200.
17. T. W. Hutchison, *On Revolutions and Progress of Economic Knowledge* (New York: Cambridge University Press, 1978) p. 57.
18. Georgescu-Roegen, *Entropy Law*, pp. 320–1.
19. J. M. Buchanan, 'Public Goods and Natural Liberty', in T. Wilson and A. Skinner (eds), *The Market and the State* (London: 1976) p. 271.
20. Allen M. Sievers, *General Economics: an Introduction* (New York: J. B. Lippincott, 1952) p. 273.
21. Robbins, *Economic Science*, pp. 19–20.
22. Ibid., p. 15.
23. Kapp, *Social Costs*, p. xxiv.
24. Adolph Lowe, *Economics and Sociology* (London: Allen & Unwin, 1935) pp. 19–22.
25. Lowe, *Economic Knowledge*, p. 13.
26. J. S. Mill, *Principles of Political Economy* in L. D. Abbott (ed.), *Masterworks of Economics* (New York: McGraw-Hill, 1973) pp. 163–4.
27. J. M. Keynes, *Essays in Persuasion* (New York: W. W. Norton, 1963) pp. 364–5.
28. William Leiss, *The Limits to Satisfaction* (University of Toronto Press, 1976).
29. Lowe, *Economic Knowledge*, p. 6.
30. Morris Bornstein, 'An Integration', in Alexander Erlich (ed.), *Comparison of Economic Systems* (Berkeley: University of California Press, 1971) p. 355.
31. Benjamin Ward, *The Socialist Economy* (New York: Random House, 1967) pp. 5–6.
32. See the review of literature in T. W. Hutchinson, *Knowledge and Ignorance in Economics* (University of Chicago Press, 1977).
33. See Neil J. Smelser, *The Sociology of Economic Life*, 2nd edn. (Englewood Cliffs, New Jersey: Prentice-Hall, 1976) p. 36.
34. See the discussion in William D. Grampp, 'Classical Economics and Its Moral Critics', *History of Political Economy*, 5 (Autumn 1972) pp. 359–74.
35. Kenneth E. Boulding, 'Economics as a Moral Science', *American Economic Review*, 59 (Mar. 1969) pp. 1–12. The quote from Wordsworth is taken from Professor Boulding's wise and beautiful article.
36. Thorstein Veblen, *The Instinct of Workmanship and the State of the Industrial Arts* (New York: A. M. Kelley, 1964) p. 25.

3 SOCIAL AND ECONOMIC INTEGRATION

1. See my 'Phenomena and Epiphenomena in Economics', *Journal of Economic Issues*, 13 (Dec. 1979) 885–98.

2. Benjamin Ward, *The Conservative Economic World View* (New York: Basic Books, 1979) p. 11.
3. J. M. Clark, *Preface to Social Economics* (New York: A. M. Kelley, 1967) p. 26.
4. C. E. Ayres, 'The Legacy of Thorstein Veblen', in Joseph Dorfman *et al.*, *Institutional Economics* (Berkeley: University of California Press, 1964) pp. 45–62.
5. See my *Economic Thought and Social Change* (Carbondale: Southern Illinois University Press, 1979) ch. 5.
6. From another publication by Sahlins, I take it that the spectrum of reciprocities originates in Elman Service, *The Hunters* (Englewood Cliffs, New Jersey: Prentice-Hall, 1966).
7. Alvin Gouldner, 'The Norm of Reciprocity: a Preliminary Statement', *American Sociological Review*, 25 (1960) p. 176.

4 THE POLITICAL ECONOMY OF MARKET CAPITALISM

1. This is actually a vast understatement which lets pass a common and grossly distorted view of the nature of mercantilism. Everyone who shares the concerns I write about in this book should read William Appleman Williams, *The Contours of American History* (New York: Franklin Watts, 1973) pp. 27–74, on British mercantilism.
2. T. W. Hutchison, *On Revolutions and Progress in Economic Knowledge* (New York: Cambridge University Press, 1978) p. 11.
3. Ibid., p. 60.
4. Benjamin Ward, *The Conservative Economic World View* (New York: Basic Books, 1979) p. 11.
5. Hutchison, *On Revolutions*, p. 45.
6. Ibid., p. 19.
7. Ibid., p. 58.
8. Ibid., p. 61n (italics omitted).
9. *Political Economy and the Philosophy of Government* (New York: A. M. Kelley, 1965) p. 115.
10. See Joyce O. Appleby, *Economic Thought and Ideology in Seventeenth Century England* (Princeton University Press, 1979).
11. See Hutchison, *On Revolutions*, p. 50; *GT*, pp. 111–12; and *PAME*, pp. 127–9.
12. See Allen M. Sievers, *General Economics: an Introduction* (New York: J. B. Lippincott, 1952) pp. 290–4.
13. See, e.g. Donald F. Gordon, 'The Role of the History of Economic Thought in the Understanding of Modern Economic Theory', *American Economic Review*, 55 (May 1955) p. 124; and A. W. Coats, 'Is there a "Structure of Scientific Revolutions" in Economics?', *Kyklos*, 22 (1969) p. 292.

5 INDUSTRIALISM AND FREEDOM

1. E. F. Schumacher, *Small is Beautiful* (New York: Harper & Row, 1973) p. 63.
2. Ibid., p. 64.
3. Ibid., p. 42.
4. Ibid., pp. 28–9.
5. Frank H. Knight, *Risk, Uncertainty and Profit* (University of Chicago Press, 1971) p. 77.
6. Ibid., p. 78.
7. Ibid., p. 79.
8. Quoted in *GT*, p. 176.
9. Karl Marx, *Grundrisse* (New York: Vintage, 1973) pp. 106–7.
10. Wendell Berry, *The Unsettling of America: Culture and Agriculture* (New York: Avon Books, 1978) p. 97.
11. Ibid., p. 43.
12. Walter Goldschmidt, *As You Sow: Three Studies in the Social Consequences of Agribusiness* (Montclair, New Jersey: Allanheld, Osmun, & Co., 1978, originally published in 1947 by The Free Press).
13. For an excellent discussion of the founding of the new American political economy see Sidney Fine, *Laissez Faire and the General–Welfare State* (Ann Arbor: University of Michigan Press, 1956) ch. 7.
14. Ibid., p. 203.
15. Ibid., p. 207n.
16. Allan G. Gruchy, *Modern Economic Thought* (New York: A. M. Kelley, 1965) pp. 620–1.
17. Walton Hamilton, *The Politics of Industry* (New York: Alfred A. Knopf, 1957) p. 6.
18. Friedrich A. Hayek, *The Road to Serfdom* (University of Chicago Press, 1944) pp. 101, 204–5.
19. Charles L. Schultze, *The Public Use of Private Interest* (Washington, DC: Brookings Institution, 1977) pp. 76–9.
20. Hamilton, *Politics of Industry*, pp. 6–7.
21. Ibid., p. 7.
22. Ibid., p. 34.
23. Ibid., p. 33.
24. Ibid., p. 29.
25. Ibid., p. 136.
26. J. K. Galbraith, *The New Industrial State* (New York: New American Library, 1968) chs 2, 3.
27. Ibid., p. 399.
28. J. K. Galbraith, *The Affluent Society* (Boston: Houghton-Mifflin, 1958) p. 100.
29. Wesley C. Mitchell, *Business Cycles* (Berkeley: University of California Press, 1913) p. 25.
30. Rexford G. Tugwell, quoted in Gruchy, *Modern Economic Thought*, p. 435.
31. Ibid., pp. 372–3.

32. Ibid., p. 570.
33. See Galbraith, *New Industrial State*, pp. vii, 381, 405 and *passim*.
34.. See J. K. Galbraith, *Economics and the Public Purpose* (Boston: Houghton-Mifflin, 1973) chs 1, 2.
35. J. M. Clark, 'The Changing Basis of Economic Responsibility', in Clark, *Preface to Social Economics* (New York: A. M. Kelley, 1967) p. 67.
36. Ibid., p. 77.
37. Schumacher, *Small is Beautiful*, p. 42.
38. Thorstein Veblen, *Absentee Ownership* (Boston: Beacon Press; 1967) pp. 65–6.
39. Thorstein Veblen, *The Vested Interests and the Common Man* (New York: Capricorn Books, 1969) p. 93.
40. Thorstein Veblen, *The Theory of Business Enterprise* (New York: New American Library, n.d.) p. 20.
41. Ibid., p. 17.
42. Galbraith, *New Industrial State*, p. 405.
43. John Dewey, *Liberalism and Social Action* (New York: Capricorn, 1963) p. 90.
44. See Gruchy, *Modern Economic Thought*, pp. 322 and 517.

Index